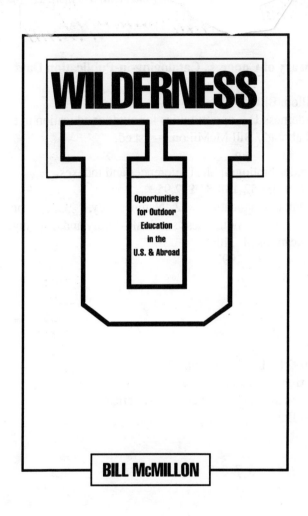

WILDERNESS U

Opportunities
for Outdoor
Education
in the
U.S. & Abroad

BILL McMILLON

CHICAGO
REVIEW
PRESS

To Bob Devine, whose article on field seminars inspired this guide

Library of Congress Cataloging-in-Publication Data

McMillon, Bill, 1942–
  Wilderness U. : opportunities for outdoor education in the U.S.
and abroad / Bill McMillon. —1st ed.
          p.   cm.
  Includes bibliographical references and indexes.
  ISBN 1-55652-158-8 : $12.95
  1. Outdoor education.   2. Nature study.   3. Environmental
education.   4. Wilderness survival—Study and teaching.
  5. Vacations. I. Title.
  LB1047.M38 1992
  371.3'8—dc20   92-19616
                                                         CIP

©1992 by Bill McMillon
All rights reserved
Printed in the United States of America
First Edition

1 2 3 4 5 6 7 8 9 10

Published in 1992 by Chicago Review Press, Incorporated
814 North Franklin Street, Chicago, Illinois 60610

Contents

The world is a beautiful book, but of little use to him who cannot read it.

—*Carlo Goldoni, 1707–93*

Introduction

The British philosopher Bertrand Russell said, "The ability to use leisure intelligently is the final test of civilization."

This is especially true today. The world has reached a turning point: we must decide whether to continue on the road to ecological destruction or turn away from such destruction to a life that emphasizes an awareness of the natural world and how to nurture nature rather than destroy it.

The eighties saw a dramatic change in the use of leisure by Americans that indicates we may be taking the turn toward a life that emphasizes an awareness of the natural world. Adventure travel, ecotourism, and similar movements led millions of tourists away from insensitive, superficial tours and days at the beach toward vacations that emphasized exploration, learning, and a renewed awareness of the natural world that surrounds us all.

Jerry Mallett of the Colorado-based marketing firm Adventure Travel Society estimates that by 1991 between 45 million and 50 million Americans engaged in some type of adventure or nature vacation activities annually. Over 25,000 companies that outfitted adventure trips of one type or another served these Americans.

Dan Taylor, professor of Recreation and Leisure Studies at San Francisco State University, says of this increasing popularity of outdoor recreation, "Recreation's true potential is just now being realized as a vehicle for personal development. More and more leisure time is being consciously utilized to help create a more whole self. The two-week vacations the families used to take to such commercial places as Disneyland or whatever are now being broken into several three- to five-day vacations of outdoor adventure."

People are gaining a better understanding of what makes them happy. They are finding that their enjoyment of outdoor activities is increased with a more thorough knowledge of the inner workings of nature.

Leisure is becoming more directly linked to a sustainable lifestyle. Work will continue to be the focal point of our society, but we are beginning to view leisure as being of critical importance to our health, happiness, and self-definition. And this is the direction leisure is headed in the nineties.

People are still flocking to Disney World, taking in rays at the beach, and filling cruise ships, but many are also exploring nature in all her varied states.

Rachel Carson wrote, "In every outthrust headland, in every curving beach, in every grain of sand, there is a story of the earth." The people who joined the adventure travel movement of the eighties and traveled to the far corners of the earth to test their skills and spirits against nature found something more. They found that they wanted to know more about the mysteries surrounding the outthrust headland, the curving beach, and the grain of sand. That desire to learn has led to the many organizations listed in this guide.

While adventure is still important to many of the millions who will enjoy the learning activities offered by these organizations, it plays second fiddle to the pursuit of knowledge. The mental stimulation offered by the structured courses and naturalist-led tours adds tremendous pleasure, as noted by one participant:

This program, above all, gave me a sense of the scientific process, and a real feel for the incredible intricacy of mother nature that can *never* be gotten from a book. Nowhere could I have gained as much understanding of the interdependence of organisms, and the fragility of that interdependence. Through the study project I found that as I learned how the tiny parts of a clock work, I gained a greater understanding and appreciation of the clock.

Although learning is often seen only as a product of formal schooling, more and more adults are using their leisure time to participate in programs such as those in this guide to increase their knowledge and appreciation of nature. In doing so, they more fully comprehend the idea that learning about nature is better done outside than in a classroom.

A report from the American Association for the Advancement of Science concerning Project 2061, an attempt to revitalize science education in America, contains a passage that best expresses this concept. Although the report was written for school-age students, it also applies to adults who are interested in pursuing their own studies outside formal schools.

The passage is from the AAAS Panel Report on the Biological and Health Sciences.

Biology is not a subject to be learned primarily from books or computerized courses, nor can it be passively acquired from viewing televised programs. It cannot be satisfactorily taught solely within the confines of the classroom even when obser- vation and experiment are emphasized. Understanding biol- ogy means being personally in touch with a living biosphere, discovering directly for oneself how it functions. It is only on the framework of personal experience with nature that class- room lessons can build. Somehow, adventures equivalent to capturing lightening bugs in jars and falling into ponds in search of frogs's eggs need to be incorporated into all our children's experiences.

How earthworms move, what happens to flies caught in a refrigerator, how spiders make webs, and the development of germinating seeds should be common knowledge for every youngster—as should the migratory patterns of local birds and the emergence sequence of plant and insect species in the spring. Once their escape from permanent entrapment in an electronic cocoon is assured, students can begin to study biology in a more formal, pedagogical way.

Substitute *person* for *youngster* and you have a statement of the purpose of this guide and the organizations listed in it. It is probably too late for you as an adult to gain those experiences in school. You need to go out on your own to expand your experiences so that slick television programs and superficial magazine articles about biology and the natural world truly make sense.

When you take that first step to study nature in nature you may closely identify with what Walt Whitman wrote in

Inscriptions: Beginning My Studies

Beginning my studies the first step pleas'd me so much,
  The mere fact consciousness, these
    forms, the power of motion,
  The least insect or animal, the senses,
    eyesight, love,
  The first step I say awed me and
    pleas'd me so much,
  I have hardly gone and hardly
    wish'd to go any farther,
  But stop and loiter all the time
    to sing it in ecstatic songs.

Begin your studies, and be sure to stop and loiter along the way, as you are awed by the very beauty and complexity of nature.

How to Use this Guide

You've decided, at least in your mind, that this year you are going to take a truly different vacation, one where you will learn new things about the natural world. You may want to learn about the Greater Yellowstone ecosystem, or about the birds of San Francisco Bay, and you know you want to do so in the two or three weeks that you have set aside for your vacation time.

Wilderness U. was written just for you, to help you decide what it is you want to study, and where you want to go to do it.

Program Guide

This sourcebook is designed to help you find the organization that most closely fits your needs. It will help you decide just how much time and effort you want to commit to learning about nature, and where you want to go to undertake your study.

Do you want to study hard your whole vacation, working in the field with nature, or would you rather spend a casual two weeks with a trained naturalist on a tour through some favorite wilderness area such as the Brooks Range of Alaska?

The organizations span the gamut from intensive, formal educational programs that take a semester or more to complete to guided tours that are led by a trained naturalist but do not require any preparation or study on the part of the participants.

What they have in common is that all or most of the time spent in the study of nature is conducted outdoors. The study of nature close up is an exciting adventure that is deeply satisfying. The intensity of the study depends strictly on your personal needs.

College and University Programs

College and university programs are closest to traditional education programs and require the most intensive study. Many are far removed from typical institutionalized colleges and universities, however, programs such as the National Audubon Society Expedition Institute, Northland College, College of the Atlantic, Prescott College, and the Huxley College of Environmental Studies at Western Washington University certainly wouldn't be familiar to anyone who studied in the 1950s.

In addition, continuing education programs where nonstudents register for off-campus classes and receive college credit have expanded tremendously in the past several decades. Today almost every two- and four-year college and university in the country offers continuing education programs that are open to everyone. Many of these include field study courses focused on an active, in-depth study of nature.

Many two- and four-year colleges also have travel/study programs that they announce in their course offerings each year.

Nature Centers and Natural History Museums

Nature centers and natural history museums are the best sources for nature education programs in many cities. Both frequently offer adult education classes, many of which are conducted outside in nature rather than in a classroom. Some also offer classes for young people.

While these courses are structured and cover a specific subject, they don't require a great deal of preparation or study time.

Field Institutes and Natural History Associations

If you know what area you want to visit and want to learn more about the natural history of the region, locate a field institute or natural history association. Many of these organizations are affiliated with a state or national park, but others are free-standing, nonprofit educational organizations that teach natural history to adults and children outside in nature.

The courses offered through these organizations are structured and cover specific subjects, but they do not require extensive study time. While courses offered by nature centers and natural history museums are often only a day or two in length, field studies are frequently up to two weeks long.

Clubs and National Associations

Many membership organizations and clubs throughout the U.S. and Canada provide nature education to their members. This can be through formal programs such as regularly scheduled seminars, tours, trips led by trained naturalists, camps of various types where participants learn about the natural history of a region, or research projects. Many of these organizations, such as the Audubon Society and the National Wildlife Federation, have broad-based programs that help educate the public about a wide range of natural history topics. Others, such as Desert Survivors, have a very narrow focus and attract members with specific interests.

Some of these programs require intensive study and preparation. Others are less demanding.

Tour Agencies and Lodges

In the past 20 years there has been an explosion of specialized travel companies and lodges that cater to travelers who wish to learn more about the natural history of a region. They often study in an informal way while taking a somewhat traditional tour. These don't make severe demands on participants but do offer them an opportunity to study a region in an informal manner.

Miscellaneous Workshops

Other workshops and classes take place outdoors in nature but do not necessarily include specific instruction about natural history. These include nature photography, climbing, canoeing, and similar workshops.

If you have a special interest and want to learn more while studying outdoors, these organizations may be the ones for you.

Programs Based in Canada and Abroad

Although many of the organizations listed in the previous section offer programs that take place outside the U.S., they are all based locally. The organizations in this section are all headquartered outside the U.S., and cater to people of all nationalities. This makes for a more eclectic group of participants, and you are less likely to meet fellow Americans on your trip.

Vignettes

This section includes a series of articles and writings by and about trip participants and leaders. These give a personalized flavor of what you will find as you join with others on a vacation at Wilderness U.

College Credits

While most adults care little about obtaining college credit for vacation study, there are some, such as teachers and college students, who are always looking for ways to pick up credits while doing something enjoyable.

Almost all programs have college credit as an option. Some, such as the colleges and universities themselves, offer credits routinely. Others, such as the field institutes and natural history museums, have ongoing contacts with local schools to offer credits for participants who desire them. If you are interested in an organization that does not have a working relationship with a college where you can obtain credit, you can generally work with the continuing education department of a college near you to obtain credit for your study.

Cross-Referenced Indexes

The cross-referenced indexes at the rear of the guide are arranged so that you can locate various organizations by a number of methods. You can search for the subjects covered in their programs or located in the regions of the world where the programs are offered.

Appendix

Finally, an appendix lists books and periodicals that frequently have information about learning and adventure vacations where participants study nature in nature.

With the information in this guide you can participate in a program that takes place in the largest classroom of all: great worldwide wilderness areas. Once you have studied the mysteries of nature in the most natural setting—nature itself—you will wonder why you ever studied anywhere other than at Wilderness U.

I

Opportunities for Outdoor Education in the U.S. and Abroad

College and University Programs

While this guide focuses on nontraditional educational activities geared toward exploring nature in nature, some of the most interesting programs available are connected with traditional colleges and universities. These institutions might be best described as semi-traditional, for the ones that offer programs where you study nature outdoors often are far removed from the standard studies of yesteryear.

Innovative environmental programs such as the National Audubon Society Expedition Institute, Northland College, College of the Atlantic, Prescott College, and the Huxley College of Environmental Studies at Western Washington University certainly wouldn't be familiar to any academic of the 1950s.

The concept of continuing education programs where nonstudents can register for off-campus classes and receive college credit is an idea that has expanded tremendously in the past several decades. Today almost every two- and four-year college and university in the country offers programs that are open to everyone, and many of these include field studies where you learn about nature in nature.

All of the programs—or almost all—in this section offer college credit for field study classes. Some even offer degrees for courses of study that are almost completely conducted in the outdoors.

If you cannot find a program in this section that covers a specific region, you can always contact several of the colleges and universities that you know are located there and see what they have in their current continuing education offerings that might meet your needs. Colleges often have one-time courses that would fit the criteria set forth for the programs in this guide, but these were not included because they do not have long-standing programs.

Many two- and four-year colleges also have travel/study programs that they announce in their course offerings each year. Santa Rosa Junior College in Santa Rosa, California, for example, has recently offered classes in the natural history of the tropical rain forests of Costa Rica during winter, spring, and summer breaks that can be taken for two or three units and cost between $1,100 and $2,400.

The entries here contain a wide range of programs, from those that offer degrees based largely on outdoor coursework to schools that provide steady groups of field study classes that are held in natural surroundings.

Appalachian Environmental Laboratory

University of Maryland Center for Environmental
and Estuarine Studies
Gunter Hall
Frostburg, MD 21532
301-689-3115

The lab established the Regional Center for Natural Science Learning to serve as an umbrella structure for all outreach programs to schools and the community. Its programs are designed to promote environmental awareness of both the state and global communities and motivate people to take an interest in the natural sciences.

As much as possible, the Learning Center's programs seek to utilize the varied natural habitats in the local Appalachian Mountains as outdoor learning sites.

Workshops for teachers, programs for gifted high-school students, field trips for the public, and master's of science programs in Wildlife Management and Fisheries Management are all offered by AEL.

Bard Graduate School of Environmental Studies

Annandale-on-Hudson, NY 12504

914-758-6822

Bard College has an unusual master's program in environmental studies. This program is offered only during the summer session and was designed to draw students from a wide variety of fields of interests and experience. The degree program takes 3 summers, and each of the first 2 is comprised of 2 4-week terms divided by a week-long reading and study period. The third summer is for thesis research.

Program activities take place on the Bard College campus, at the Ecology Field Station adjacent to the 1,400-acre Tivoli Bay Wildlife Management Area (a part of the Hudson River National Estuarine Research Reserve) and the 3,600-acre Black Rock Forest Preserve at Cornwall, New York.

The program costs about $6,500 per summer, which includes room and board. Students with spouses and/or children must find off-campus housing.

Boulder Outdoor Survival School, Inc.

PO Box 905
Rexburg, ID 83440

208-356-7446

This is not a traditional college program, but it can be taken for college credit through cooperative agreements with several universities.

The school instructs students with hands-on learning activities, maintains a low student-teacher ratio, and guarantees results. Students learn to survive with the land and cope with the elements. The school believes that one "learns not to fight nature, but to cooperate. She is impartial, but not forgiving."

Practical knowledge comes from experience. Natives from all parts of the world have learned to live in balance with earth and spirit in order to survive.

BOSS challenges men, women, and young adults to face life and survive on their own initiative, without the conveniences and premanufactured gadgets of civilization. Survival in any land in any circumstance demands courage and commitment. With this in mind, BOSS is dedicated to the instruction and preservation of primitive survival arts and the development of the individual through experience with the natural world and aboriginal tradition.

They do this through skills courses, where basic survival techniques are taught at a field base camp, and in walkabouts, where students live what they learn in harsh, primitive situations.

Courses are offered in Utah and Idaho, last from 5 to 27 days, and cost between $400 and $1,200.

College credit is available through cooperative agreements BOSS has with several local universities.

California State Polytechnic University
3801 West Temple Avenue
Pomona, CA 91768

714-869-2288

A group of science professors from Cal Poly began leading a travel/study tour of Venezuela in the mid-eighties. This 2-week trip is led by Cal Poly professors and experienced local guides through diverse ecological zones of the country. The trip was designed to introduce participants to a variety of tropical environments from the Caribbean Coast to the heart of the tropical rain forests.

Participants have the opportunity to snorkel along the coral reefs, hike in the cloud forests and lowland rain forests, and see unique fish and hundreds of bird species as they move from habitat to habitat.

The trip may be taken for 3 units of undergraduate credit and costs about $3,000, which includes round-trip airfare from Los Angeles.

Catalina Science Semester
University of Southern California
University Park
Los Angeles, CA 90089-0371

213-740-5800

The Department of Biological Science at the University of Southern California offers a special program each spring on Catalina Island. Although designed for biological science and pre-med majors, others may apply for the 35 spaces in the program. Students take 4 upper-division biology classes during the semester. These are arranged in a format that creates a logical, focused, and effective presentation of the biological sciences at an advanced undergraduate level. The courses proceed from an initial ecological process-oriented beginning, through an organismal, life-history-concerned intermediate, to a final, more reductionist, physiological and biochemical level of analysis.

During each unit, 3 weeks are devoted to formal classroom instruction followed by 9 days of directed research, much of which takes place outdoors.

Registration must be made prior to November 1 each fall. Cost per semester is approximately $10,000. Financial aid may be available.

Cornell Laboratory of Ornithology
159 Sapsucker Woods Road
Ithaca, NY 14850
607-254-2404

This lab, which is connected with Cornell University—and sits adjacent to it—offers special workshops in various aspects of birding each year. Recent workshops have included natural-sound recording techniques and birding-by-ear workshops in the Sierra Nevada at San Francisco State University's Sierra Nevada Field Research Campus in Sattley, California.

These courses can be taken on credit or noncredit bases, last 7 days, and cost $550 for noncredit and $740 for credit.

Other workshops are offered by the lab, and travel/study programs as well.

Cornell's Adult University
626B Thurston Avenue
Ithaca, NY 14850-2490
607-255-6260

Two separate programs are available through the Adult University education vacations. The first are 7- to 17-day trips led by Cornell professors to various sites around the world. Not all of these trips have a natural history orientation, but some have, such as Belizean Ecologies from the Highlands to the Sea; Natural Life of the Everglades, Corkscrew Swamp, and Big Cypress Preserve; New Orleans, the Gulf Coast, and the Bayous; and Culture and Ecology

Most students like to get their feet and hands wet as they study swamp life. (*Photo courtesy of Cornell Adult University*)

of the Chesapeake. Costs for these trips range between $1,000 and $2,500, and no credit is available.

Another program through the Adult University is Summer CAU where about 150 adults, plus an equal number of children, spend a week on campus at Cornell attending special morning classes and enjoying free time every afternoon. Separate programs are offered for adults and youth, and selections in each include field studies where students learn about nature in nature.

These courses cost about $700 including room and board for adults and $300 for youth. No credit is available.

Elderhostel
75 Federal Street, Suite 400
Boston, MA 02110
617-426-7788

Elderhostel Canada
33 Prince Arthur Avenue, Suite 300
Toronto, ON M5R 1B2 Canada
416-964-2260

Elderhostel began in 1975 when colleges, universities, research institutes, and museums throughout Canada and the U.S. became convinced that the young should not be the only ones who could enjoy the advantages of education and travel. A series of 1-week courses for senior citizens over the age of 60 was offered under the auspices of Elderhostel. Participants stayed in student housing, ate in student cafeterias, and had all the privileges of extracurricular activities being offered on campus. Three subjects were offered in each program, and participants could choose to take 1 to 3 courses during the week.

Course offerings are now very wide-ranging, and many cover natural history topics where participants learn in the field. Elderhostel has programs at educational institutions around the world.

Programs in the U.S. and Canada last for 1 week, while the international programs last for 3 to 4 weeks. U.S. and Canadian programs cost between $225 and $800, and international programs cost between $1,000 and $6,000.

This is a restricted program where participants must be at least 60 years of age, although companions over the age of 50 may accompany those over 60.

Contact Elderhostel for current offerings.

Environmental Studies Program

University of Hawaii at Manoa
Crawford 317
2550 Campus Road
Honolulu, HI 96822

808-956-7361

This program is an individual academic designation under the auspices of the Liberal Studies Program. Participants may either pursue a major in environmental studies or a certificate in environmental studies that augments other academic majors. The program encourages self-direction and allows students to design their own curricula. This may entail considerable fieldwork.

An internship involving hands-on work in an environmental agency is required for both the major and the certificate.

The university also offers some continuing education courses where students study nature in the great outdoors.

Field Studies by the Sea

College of the Atlantic
105 Eden Street
Bar Harbor, ME 04609

207-288-5015

Established in 1981, this program provides introductory through advanced course work in environmental subjects and the life sciences. It is primarily for elementary and high-school teachers although others may attend.

Courses emphasize field trips that take advantage of the 150 square miles of coastal mountains, forests, fields, and wetlands of Acadia National Park. They also utilize the surrounding bays, estuaries, beaches, and open oceans for marine study. All or part of these courses take place aboard the 95-foot schooner *Harvey Gamage*.

Three 2-week sessions are held each summer, with each focusing on different topics. Three graduate credits are available from the College of the Atlantic and the University of Maine for each course.

Costs are about $250 per unit and $200 per week for room and board. Courses that utilize the *Harvey Gamage* cost between $275 and $400 extra.

Field Studies in Natural History
San Jose State University
Biological Science Department
San Jose, CA 95192-0135
408-924-2625

This program includes a number of courses year-round where complete families can participate. The courses were developed primarily for teachers, but anyone can attend.

Past courses have included Death Valley in the Spring, North Coast of California, and Volcanoes to the Sea.

The family participation plan allows spouses to take part in the class without credit at a reduced rate, and summer session classes have a concurrent junior program for children aged 6 to 16.

Courses cost about $150 for 1 week.

Glen Helen Outdoor Education Center
Antioch University
1075 South Route 343
Yellow Springs, OH 45387
513-767-7648

This center has 10 naturalist/intern positions open for 5-month terms each August and January for people interested in obtaining experience and college credit while working with school groups. All interns receive either 10 graduate or 12 undergraduate credits for extensive ongoing training, reading, and projects.

Another branch of Antioch University—Antioch New England Graduate School, Keene, New Hampshire, 03431; 603-357-3122—offers the largest, most diversified professional training program in the Northeast for those interested in environmental leadership. An M.S. degree is offered in both Environmental

Studies and in Resource Management. Classes in both programs are scheduled so that students can continue to work while pursuing their degree.

Hawaii Loa College
45-045 Kam Highway
Kaneohe, HI 96744
808-235-3641

A 3-unit, 20-day field study course entitled Hawaiian Environmental History is offered several times a year at Hawaii Loa College. This course is taught by Zane Bilgrav, owner and operator of Pacific Quest Outdoor Adventures (see listing in Tour Agencies section).

Hawaii Loa College is located on Oahu, but only the first 2 and last 4 days are spent on campus. The other days are spent exploring the islands of Kauai, Molokai, Maui, and Hawaii.

Higgins Lake Environmental School
104 Conservation Drive
Roscommon, MI 48653
517-821-6200

This school has offered courses for teachers, 4-H and scout leaders, public officials, environmental group members, and graduate students since 1946. The program was started to provide a better understanding of the relationship between humans and their environment in these changing times.

Resource people, material, lectures, field trips, and discussions all focus on understanding critical issues dealing with the above relationship.

Courses are offered for university credit or audit and cost between $90 and $300 plus room and board. Room and board are provided by the MacMullan Conference Center for about $2,110 per session.

Huxley College of Environmental Studies

Western Washington University
Bellingham, WA 98225

206-676-3520

Huxley College began in the fall of 1970 as an attempt by students and faculty to develop a program that revolved around *ecology*, a curriculum that had never yet been attempted. This was in a time when even the word was unfamiliar to most academics, much less to the general public.

Huxley developed a hands-on style that was unusual in those days and has since spread across the country and around the world. You don't go to Huxley and expect to sit in lectures and be told what you need to know, according to a dean of the college. Instead, you are given information and concepts in methodology and skill in a variety of ways of investigating and are made to apply them on your own.

One part of the program is its Spring Block. This is an 11-week field quarter that uses experiential learning and outdoor adventure education techniques. Students enroll for a block of classes (Outdoor Education, Environmental Education, Adventure Programming and Leadership, Experiential Learning in Environmental Education, and The Writing of American Naturalists), most of which are taught outdoors. Rock climbing, winter camping, wilderness travel, and ecology are all taught during extensive field trips. All environmental education majors at the college must take this Spring Block.

B.A., B.S., M.S., and M.A. degrees are all offered through the school, as are a number of continuing education courses.

Institute for Environmental Studies

University of Washington
Engineering Annex FM-12
Seattle, WA 98195
206-543-1812

This institute has developed undergraduate and graduate environmental curricula that encourage interdisciplinary research and public service programs that include continuing education.

Most of the courses taught at the institute supplement student studies in other departments or are offered in its Continuing Environmental Education Program. This program conducts conferences, seminars, public forums, and short courses on environmental topics.

For information about current offerings and costs, contact the institute.

Interhostel

University of New Hampshire
6 Garrison Avenue
Durham, NH 03824-3529
603-862-1147
800-733-9753
FAX 603-862-1113

This program was modeled after Elderhostel but offered international trips at a time when Elderhostel was limited to the U.S. and Canada. The latter now offers both international and domestic programs, but Interhostel is still internationally oriented.

This university-sponsored travel/study program covers a wide range of topics, and natural history, field study programs are an integral part of the offerings.

Participants in Interhostel must be at least 50 years of age, although companions may be 40 or older. Programs last between 2 and 3 weeks and cost between $1,100 and $1,900.

The International Honors Program

19 Braddock Park
Boston, MA 02116

617-267-8612

The International Honors Program was founded in 1958 in cooperation with Bard College to offer students an unequaled opportunity to study overseas. Each year's itinerary is global and involves comparative study of several contrasting societies. For the past several years, global ecology has been the focus of the program as students studied in England, India, Thailand, Malaysia, New Zealand, Colombia, and the United States.

Thirty students are selected to participate in the program each year, and all carry a full load of 5 courses each semester for a total of 32 semester units through Bard College. Guest lecturers and field study play a major role in the curriculum.

There are no specific prerequisites for the program, and although most participants are either college students or recent graduates the student age range has been between 18 and 56 years.

The Global Ecology curriculum examines ways of understanding the Earth and its inhabitants as a single complex system and considers patterns of action within the context of global ecology. The program was developed by Edward Goldsmith, Director of the Wadebridge Ecological Centre in Cornwall, England, and publisher and senior editor of *The Ecologist* magazine. He is joined on the faculty by an international team of experts.

Classes meet 4 days a week, students generally live with families in each country, and the cost of the program is about $19,000 for the year. This includes all air and land transportation in the itinerary, room and board, books, and tuition. Some financial assistance is available.

Iowa Lakeside Laboratory
RR 2, PO Box 305
Milford, IA 51351

712-337-3669

This field station, located in the lakes region of northwest Iowa, is sponsored jointly by Iowa State University, the University of Northern Iowa, and the University of Iowa. It sits on 140 acres of grassland and gallery forest adjacent to Miller's Bay on the west shore of West Okoboji Lake.

The lab was established in 1909 and was the earliest local attempt to provide a place where the rich flora and fauna of the northern Iowa lake and prairie regions could be studied and conserved.

The lab provides a special opportunity for serious biology students (undergraduates, graduates, and advanced amateurs) to investigate plants and animals in their natural systems. The summer program enables students to concentrate on these studies in a way not possible during the regular year.

Habitats that can be studied range from high morainic knobs to lakes and kettle holes, and these support a wide range of plant communities. Deep ravines support hanging bogs, and on the nearby prairies there are alkaline and acid fens.

The lab does not grant degrees, but courses taken during the summer sessions are given for credit. The sessions last for 4 weeks, and you may take 1 course per session for a maximum of 5 credits. The first session generally begins the first week in June and goes through the first week of July, and the second session follows immediately and goes through the first or second week of August.

Costs for each session are about $500, plus another $450 for room and board. Special arrangements can be made for family cottages.

National Audubon Society Expedition Institute

PO Box 170
Readfield, ME 04355
207-685-3111

This has to be the most nontraditional college program in the country. Students can earn a hands-on B.S. or M.S. degree while traveling by van throughout the U.S. and Canada. This degree program is offered through Lesley College Graduate School of Cambridge, Massachusetts, in cooperation with the National Audubon Society.

The B.S. degree in Environmental Education consists of 2 years of general education courses with Lesley or any other accredited college or university and 2 years with the Audubon Expedition Institute.

The 2-year M.S. degree in Environmental Education consists of 3 semesters of field studies and 1 semester of internship or a research thesis.

AEI sees the movable classroom concept of expedition education as a viable alternative to traditional programs and as a course of study that provides not just theory, but hands-on learning experience in a setting where individuals are responsible for action.

Course work is interwoven with outdoor and travel experiences that explore a wealth of environments from New England forests, mountains, and shores; Native American communities; Florida Everglades and river systems; and western mountain wilderness areas; to southwestern deserts. The courses are issue-oriented, reflecting in their studies and approach current environmental, ecosocial, and ecopolitical concerns. All instructors have at least an M.S. in Environmental Education and have broad experience in the field.

Students learn to understand ecological systems, increase their versatility, and prepare themselves for occupations in a variety of environmental settings.

Courses are offered at the high-school, undergraduate, and graduate levels.

The high-school and undergraduate courses may be taken as either degree or nondegree programs. For nondegree programs, students may enroll for either a semester or a full year. Credits are fully transferable to other colleges and universities.

The high-school programs cost $5,500 for 1 semester or $9,300 for a full year. The undergraduate programs cost the same, with an extra $1,312-per-semester tuition to Lesley College for an accredited degree.

The 2-year graduate program costs $9,300 per year, with an extra $1,968 per year to Lesley College for an accredited degree.

AEI and Lesley College offer a number of grants and sholarships to assist students with tuition costs.

National Outdoor Leadership School

Box AA
Lander, WY 82520-0579
307-332-6973
FAX 307-332-3631

The National Outdoor Leadership School has taught wilderness skills, conservation, and leadership to over 30,000 students since 1965.

Notebooks and pencils are as vital as climbing ropes or ice axes on a NOLS course as skills and information essential to low-impact wilderness living are presented in a wide variety of ways. Students are taught to be safe and knowledgeable users of the wilderness as they examine the wildlife, flora, weather, and geology of their surroundings.

"What I hear, I forget; what I see, I remember; what I do, I know" is the Chinese proverb that mirrors NOLS's teaching philosophy. Education is the school's priority, and the instructors believe that the best wilderness education comes through experience.

All instructors are carefully selected, thoroughly trained, and love to teach. They may be a doctor of botany, a mountaineer with multiple ascents in the Himalayas, or a former ski patroller, but all are backcountry experts that teach self-contained courses where the wilderness is the classroom and the surrounding environment is course material.

Many of the more than 40 courses offered at NOLS in their branch schools in Wyoming, Arizona, Washington, Alaska, Mexico, Kenya, and Chile include rock climbing, kayaking, and other adventure/travel activities. Yet this is not a travel company that offers guides for your comfort and convenience; they don't do for you, but teach you to do for yourself. Students learn how to make decisions, evaluate hazards, and be responsible for themselves and each other.

NOLS has courses in wilderness, water, winter, and mountaineering activities, as well as instruction for educators. Sessions last from 10 days to 3 months, and all are demanding of students as they learn to participate in rigorous outdoor activities in a safe manner. Since physical activity is such an integral part of each course, all students must have a physical exam prior to enrollment.

College credit can be earned through the University of Utah. Tuition is about $70 to $80 per day, with most courses costing between $1,000 and $3,000, and semester courses costing up to $6,500. Financial aid is available for those who show potential to forward the school's mission and who would not be able to attend a course without assistance.

Northland College
Ashland, WI 54806
715-682-1699

This small liberal arts/environmental college was established in 1892 along the shores of Lake Superior as the North Wisconsin Academy, and it has maintained its small liberal arts reputation for a full century. Today it has incorporated *environmental* into its name as a sign that its students will gain an understanding of the world's natural surroundings during their education there.

This environmentally conscious emphasis is apparent from the presentation of the college catalog and informational brochures, where photos of students working and studying in the outdoors predominate, to the orientation sessions for freshmen and transfer

Biology students identify specimens collected from an outdoor laboratory in far northern Wisconsin. (*Photo courtesy of Don Albrecht*)

students. These orientations are 5-day and 4-night sessions in the primitive Northwoods where students get to know about Northland College as they become involved in hands-on outdoor activities led by upperclassmen.

After students become involved, they find that environmental studies and outdoor education are popular majors and that these sections cross over to other majors as well.

Yearly costs at Northland are about $11,000, and financial aid is available.

As part of the college's community-outreach program, as many as 200 educational seminars and workshops on issues of concern to the North Country are presented by the Sigurd Olson Environmental Institute each year. This institute was conceived with the idea that it could increase public understanding of the interrelationships between society and the natural world.

Interpretive courses on the Apostle Islands National Lakeshore and other natural history subjects are offered through continuing education programs.

The 13-day writing-adventure program called Wordscapes: Writing and the World of Nature is another popular program offered by the college. This program brings leading writers together with students of all ages to explore the major outdoor writing genres. Mornings are devoted to lectures and afternoons are planned for outdoor experiences.

A major portion of the program involves a 4-day canoe, kayak, or sailing adventure to the Apostle Islands.

Cost for this program is about $750 including room and board.

For a more graphic depiction of the Wordscapes itenerary, see "Wordscapes—Northland College's Outdoor Writing Institute Takes Shape" in the Vignettes section.

Outdoor Semester in the Rockies

Timberline Campus
901 South Highway 24
Colorado Mountain College
Leadville, CO 80461

719-486-2015

Outdoor Semester in the Rockies blends the best of outdoor adventure with classic disciplines of college education. The program directors believe that the education of the whole person is important and that academic training is far more effective if it is balanced with experiences that help you grow physically and personally. The Outdoor Semester gives you that balance.

Traditional academic and liberal arts courses such as science and philosophy are taught in the mountains, the desert, and the snow where participants learn how to adapt to different conditions and how to care for each fragile environment.

During the semester, participants move from sections in Mountaineering, Southwestern Studies, Mexican Travel, and Rock Climbing, to Ice Climbing and High Angle Snow Travel, Avalanche Studies, Telemark/Nordic Skiing, and Winter Camping and Backcountry Skiing. In all these the students are guided by highly qualified outdoor educators who are at home in the classroom as well as in the field. All instructors combine excellent academic credentials with years of experience teaching in an outdoor setting. Visiting lecturers also make presentations to the classes.

Participants who complete the semester receive 18 units of credit. The cost for the semester is amazingly little. In-state residents pay $675 plus books and personal equipment and out-of-state residents pay $2,250 plus books and personal equipment. Financial aid is available for those eligible.

For more detailed information about this program, refer to the article "The Chance of a Lifetime" in the Vignettes section.

Prescott College

220-B Grove Avenue
Prescott, AZ 86301

602-778-2090

A number of years ago Prescott College was a small, financially troubled liberal arts college that was in threat of bankruptcy. A group of professors, students, and others took over the program and made it an alternative to more traditional arts colleges. Through their efforts the college has developed an innovative liberal arts program that emphasizes environmental studies and uses the Southwest, from the Sea of Cortez to the Grand Canyon, as its classroom.

With small classes that involve extensive fieldwork and an opportunity for participants to design their own educational path, Prescott has drawn a student body that is actively involved with the learning process, and one that is environmentally aware.

The campus is located in the mountains of central Arizona, but the students can be found around the world during the school year—learning about nature and the environment firsthand.

School of Natural Resources

University of Vermont
Aiken Center
Burlington, VT 05405

802-656-4280

The School of Natural Resources is a small college within a comprehensive university that uses teaching in the outdoors to provide students with an understanding of the structure, dynamics, and conservation of natural ecosystems, and an appreciation of the importance of maintaining a healthy environment. Although much of the program involves traditional classroom instruction, students can spend considerable time outdoors in natural laboratories studying ecology.

The school also offers some programs that are open to the public.

 ## *Shaver Creek Environmental Center*
The Pennsylvania State University
203 Henderson Building South
University Park, PA 16802
814-863-2000

This center is dedicated to education and research in the fields of recreation and parks and environmental interpretation. It not only provides outstanding recreational opportunities in central Pennsylvania, but also educational experiences in a number of other fields. The center offers access to 1,000 acres of hemlock and oak woodlands, meandering streams, open meadows, cattail marshes, and a 72-acre lake.

Family, adult, and child programs open to the public are offered year-round. Topics vary with the season, and include intern programs at the outdoor school, discovery walks, a ropes and cooperation course, and natural history seminars. Costs are minimal.

Sheldon Jackson College
801-B Lincoln Street
Sitka, AK 99835
907-747-5221

This small 2-year college sits on the shores of Alaska's Island Passage and offers students an opportunity to study marine biology and natural resources in an unsurpassed setting. The college uses the Pacific Ocean and the world's largest temperate rain forest as its classrooms, and all who study there understand how John Muir appreciated his respites on the campus during several of his Alaskan adventures.

Shoals Marine Laboratory
G-14Y Stimson Hall
Cornell University
Ithaca, NY 14853
607-255-3717

This marine research station is cosponsored by Cornell University and the University of New Hampshire and sits on 95-acre Appledore Island, 6 miles off the shores of Maine and New Hampshire. Appledore is a pristine refuge for a variety of wildlife, and an unsullied classroom for those who wish to study marine life. The station is one of the premier research and teaching facilities in the country, and top experts take classes on expeditions to bird rookeries, tidal pools, out to sea, or underwater to study marine life.

Two categories of classes are offered at the lab. The first consists of classes designed for college credit. These are attended primarily by students who are pursuing a degree, and most have prerequisites. The second involves noncredit classes open to everyone, regardless of expertise or previous academic standing.

Credit courses include such topics as Adaptations of Marine Organisms, Field Marine Science, and Marine Biology for Teachers. Noncredit courses include Nature Photography by the Sea; Birds, Islands, and the Sea; Marine and Coastal Geology; and A Sea Beside the Sea: Ecology of the Gulf of Maine.

Credit courses last between 7 and 21 days and cost $550 to $2,000. Noncredit courses last between 2 and 6 days and cost $115 to $750.

Many of the noncredit courses are advertised through Cornell's Adult University (see listing).

Smoky Mountain Field School

University of Tennessee, Noncredit Programs
600 Henley Street, Suite 105
Knoxville, TN 37902

615-974-0150
800-284-8885

The school provides intensive 1-, 2-, and 5-day field seminars emphasizing outdoor exploration of the Smoky Mountains. Some courses are complemented by classroom activities. The program is sponsored jointly by the Great Smoky Mountain National Park and the University of Tennessee. Seminars are taught by professors and naturalists who live in the region and have spent considerable time studying the natural history of the Smoky Mountains.

Seminars cost between $30 and $195. Participants are responsible for making their own arrangements for room and board unless otherwise specified in the course description.

Sport Fishing School

North Carolina State University
Department of Zoology
Office of Continuing Education
Raleigh, NC 27695-7401

919-737-2261

Since the early 1950s the university has offered a fishing school at Hatteras, North Carolina, for anglers who want to learn more about fishing for offshore big-game fish. This school is open to anyone who is interested in sport fishing, although those under 16 years of age must be accompanied by an adult participant.

Instructors in this 1-week school include tackle representatives, conservation experts, fisheries scientists, and university staff members.

In-classroom lectures are held on shore some mornings, and 2 days are spent fishing aboard boats in the Gulf Stream off Cape Hatteras. Other days are spent sound, pier, and surf fishing. Lec-

A group of triumphant participants display the fruits of Sport Fishing School. (*Photo courtesy of North Carolina State University*)

tures cover techniques of all types of fishing and much about the marine ecology of the region.

The cost for the 5-day course is $700, which does not include lodging.

In the late 1980s, the university began offering a second sport fishing school at Walker's Cay Resort in Abaco, Bahamas. This school is very similar to the one at Hatteras except for the tropical environment.

The cost of the 7-day, 6-night program is $1,500, which includes lodging, meals, and flight from Ft. Lauderdale, Florida. Anyone under 18 years of age must be accompanied by an adult participant.

Another program at North Carolina State University that offers students an opportunity to study nature in nature is in the Department of Forestry (919-737-2891). Many courses in the program include lab sections that are taught outdoors, and all students in the program are required to complete a 10-week, 10-unit summer camp that is taught entirely in the field at one of the college's forests.

Texas Tech University Center at Junction
PO Box 186
Junction, TX 76849
915-446-2301

This off-campus center of Texas Tech University sits on over 400 acres in the Hill Country of central Texas. It is nestled along the bottom land of the south fork of the spring-fed Llano River where juniper-covered hillsides join with native pecan groves.

A variety of courses are offered at this field-station–type branch of the main campus, most of which are in biology, including field ecology. Most students at the center are degree-seeking students from Texas Tech, but anyone may enroll for the credit courses.

Noncredit retreats and workshops of various types are held at the center year-round, and a full complement of courses are offered during the summer.

Costs for the courses vary but generally run about $100 per unit for Texas residents and $175 per unit for nonresidents. Room and board cost approximately $25 per day.

Touch the Earth Outdoor Program
Division of Recreational Services
The University of Iowa
Iowa City, IA 52242
319-335-9293

The Division of Recreational Services at the University of Iowa was designed to appeal to the general student population and to give everyone an opportunity for enjoying outdoor activities. Kayaking, bicycling, rock climbing, backpacking, scuba diving, cross-country skiing, and fishing are just some of the activities the program offers. These take place from Wyoming to Georgia.

Most activities last between 2 and 3 days, but an occasional session lasts for 10 days. They cost between $50 and $375.

This program is open to the general public at the same fee structure as for students.

University of Montana
Missoula, MT 59812-1002
406-243-5122 (Flathead Lake)
406-243-5361 (Wilderness Institute)
FAX 406-243-4184

There are several programs offered through different divisions of the university that are appropriate for this guide. The first is the Flathead Lake Biological Field Station, which is located on 160 acres at Yellow Bay on the east shore of the lake, some 70 miles north of the Missoula campus. This field station operates as a research site year-round and as a summer academic center. As many as 110 students can board at the station for the 8-week summer session that is offered annually.

Flathead Lake is located amid some of the most beautiful wilderness in North America, and participants at the station spend their free hours hiking and backpacking into Glacier National Park and the Great Bear and Bob Marshall wilderness areas, or fishing in Flathead or other lakes, rivers, and streams in the region.

Formal courses that emphasize field investigations of the rich flora and fauna of both aquatic and terrestrial habitats found near the station (aquatic studies are featured, however) are offered for both graduate and undergraduate students. Faculty from both the University of Montana and other universities across the U.S. and Canada provide instruction for courses that meet for 8 hours a day 2 days per week.

Students must have completed introductory courses in biology, botany, zoology, and chemistry before enrolling.

Students live in summer cabins that are scattered along the lake shoreline or in a new dormitory. Students and faculty dine together in the Prescott Center. Tuition for 14 to 18 quarter units is about

$550 for Montana residents and $650 for nonresidents, and room and board ranges from $850 to $1,000.

The second is the Wilderness Institute in the School of Forestry. The School of Forestry offers a Wilderness Studies minor that is designed to produce informed citizens that are better able to participate in processes for public involvement concerning wilderness issues. An integral part of the minor is the Wilderness and Civilization program that uses over 5 million acres of wilderness in the Wild Rockies Bioregion as a classroom. This is a unique interdisciplinary academic program designed to educate a select group of undergraduate students in the values, problems, and promises of wilderness. Participation in the program consists of 2 semesters of academic classes, 2 extended backpacking treks, and other field trips and group activities. The program focuses on understanding wilderness and wildlands and their relationship to contemporary American society by integrating the humanities, sciences, and social sciences. The course runs mid-September through mid-May for two semesters. Cost per semester is about $800 in-state, and $2,000 for out-of-staters.

The third is the Bison Range Discovery Workshop for Teachers that is offered through the Center for Continuing Education (c/o National Bison Range, Moiese, MT 59824; 406-644-2211). This 1-day workshop is offered in both the fall and spring, and participants choose from several seminars that are offered each session. These seminars are led by expert naturalists who lead participants in hands-on learning activities. All participants also receive a copy of *The National Bison Range: A Classroom Without Walls* activity guide. Costs for these seminars are minimal.

For a vivid account of the Wilderness and Civilization experience, see "The University of Wild" in the Vignettes section.

University of North Carolina
Campus Box 2100, Hanes Hall
Chapel Hill, NC 27599-2100

Although this university offers no information on specific courses about nature taught in nature, it does provide graduate programs in Ecology and Marine Sciences. For those interested in Marine Sciences, ocean-oriented courses are available through the departmental, curriculum, and summer sessions offerings for students not necessarily preparing for graduate study.

Interested individuals might want to check out what is offered to people not enrolled in a program at the school.

White Mesa Institute
College of Eastern Utah
639 West 1st South 50-1
Blanding, UT 84511

801-678-2220

This institute offers an array of educational trips and workshops in the Four Corners area. Although most of these cover prehistoric and contemporary cultures of the region, some cover natural history, specifically as it relates to the cultural history there.

All programs are taught outdoors or have a strong field complement to an indoor workshop.

Workshops last between 2 and 8 days and cost between $200 and $800. Lodging and food is included for some of the programs, but not for others.

College credit is available for most workshops.

Wilderness Studies Program

University of Alaska, Anchorage
3211 Providence Drive
Anchorage, AK 99508

907-786-1468

This program offers interdisciplinary studies and field study programs that are open to both degree and nondegree students. Field study programs utilize the vast wilderness areas of Alaska as their classrooms.

Wildland Studies

San Francisco State University
3 Mosswood Circle
Cazadero, CA 95421

707-632-5665

Participants join backcountry study teams as working field associates with Wildland Studies. They help qualified researchers search for answers to important environmental problems involving wildlife, wildlands, and wildwater projects in the mountains of the western U.S., Alaska, Hawaii, New Zealand, Canada, Thailand, and Nepal.

The projects take place completely in the field with long days and uphill on trails in weather conditions that are not always ideal.

Participants learn about research techniques and the subject under study as they work side-by-side with project leaders and can earn 3 units of upper-division credits from San Francisco State University per project.

Projects that earn 3 credits are from 14 to 18 days and cost about $425, and those that earn 9 units are for 6 weeks and cost $825. International projects are considerably more expensive.

Nature Centers and Natural History Museums

Nature centers and natural history museums are the best sources for nature education programs in many cities. Both frequently offer adult education classes, many of which are conducted outside rather than in a classroom. Some also offer classes for young people.

Most of the classes offered through nature centers and natural history museums concentrate on local events and places. Some of the larger museums also offer travel/study programs where you go some distance from home to study natural history. Registration is seldom restricted to members or local residents, and these offerings are an excellent way to become intimately acquainted with the natural history of a region, even one far from home. A majority of classes are very short—an evening, a day, or two at the most. Field trips are somewhat longer, but seldom over a week.

Many of the courses offered through natural history museums can be taken for credit through colleges and universities providing cooperative programs. For more information about this, contact the museum of your choice. If they do not have a cooperative program with a local college or university, you can often work through a college near you.

To obtain current listings of courses and field trips, contact the programs that seem to cover the subjects or regions that you are interested in studying.

The Academy of Natural Sciences of Philadelphia

19th and Parkway, Logan Square
Philadelphia, PA 19103

r215-299-1054

The academy offers courses and expeditions for adults and children, most of which are concerned with the natural history of Pennsylvania and surrounding states, but some are as far away as Florida and the Pacific Northwest.

A special field program offered by the academy is the Marine Island Ecology program at the Hardwood Island Biological Station in Maine. This program is for high-school students with a genuine interest in ecological and environmental studies. There are few classroom sessions as nearly all instruction is carried out in forests, fields, lakes, and oceans.

Any student who has completed the sophomore year of high school and a course in general, life, or physical science can apply. Two sessions are offered each summer, each with a maximum of 16 students. The program costs $850 for applications made before April 15, and $900 thereafter. Some scholarships are available.

Austin Nature Center

301 Nature Center Drive
Austin, TX 78746

512-327-8181

The nature center offers outings that range from half-day hikes to week-long trips to natural areas around Austin and throughout Texas. These are for both children and adults.

Breazeale Interpretive Center

Padilla Bay National Estuarine Research Center
1043 Bayview-Edison Road
Mount Vernon, WA 98273

206-428-1558

The center offers a number of 1- and 2-day courses and programs year-round, with college credit available for many.

Cabrillo Marine Museum

3720 Stephen White Drive
San Pedro, CA 90731

213-548-7562 (recorded message)

The Cabrillo Museum is dedicated to promoting knowledge and awareness of the marine life of Southern California and does so through a number of educational programs.

The best of these programs is a series of Science at the Seashore courses that are offered on weekends year-round. These include tidepool walks, discovery seminars, art at the ocean, crab watches, mud walks, and bird talks.

Costs for these are between $1 and $60. Call the museum for a recorded message about this season's offerings.

California Academy of Sciences
Golden Gate Park
San Francisco, CA 94118
415-750-7100

Workshop members study a sand dune as the surf pounds on the beach below.
(*Photo by Caroline Copp, courtesy of the California Academy of Sciences*)

The oldest natural history museum in the West, the Academy of
Sciences offers a full line of adult and children's field study
programs throughout the year. These cover many areas of the west
in addition to the San Francisco Bay region. It also sponsors a
number of travel and adventure-travel programs.

Contact them for their current offerings.

The Catskill Center for Conservation and Development, Inc.
Arkville, NY 12406-9989

914-586-2611
FAX 914-586-3044

This center is an advocate for environmental causes in the Catskill region and offers technical workshops for local and regional planners and government officials on environmental issues.

It also offers a number of field trips and excursions for the general public during the year. Some recent sessions have included Hudson River Evening Cruise—A Natural and Cultural History of the Catskills and the Hudson, Family Nature Walk at Alder Lake, and Sundays in the Park—Bike Rides Through Catskill Park.

Cost for these is between $5 and $20.

Center for Environmental Study
143 Bostwick NE
Grand Rapids, MI 49503

616-771-3935
FAX 616-771-4005

The center, which is headquartered on the campus of Grand Rapids Community College, is a nonprofit organization that is devoted to helping preserve and enhance the quality of the global environment through education, communication, and research.

One part of the program provides summer seminars, primarily for teachers, but open to other interested parties, entitled Teaching With the Earth. Another leads ecology study trips in Costa Rica, Kenya, the Galapagos, and Ecuador.

Costs vary from about $50 for the teacher summer seminars to over $3,000 for the study trips to Kenya. Reservations for the study trips are handled by Voyagers International (listed in Tour Agencies).

Circle Pines Center

8560 Mullen Road
Delton, MI 49046

616-623-5555

Workshops, retreats, classes, and camps are all offered at this cooperative educational and recreational center. The purpose of the center is to demonstrate cooperative alternatives for economic and social issues and to teach cooperation as a way of life. Natural history and environmentally conscious cooperation are part of the instruction.

There are special youth, adult, family, and elder camps each summer.

Rates are from $5 to $42 per day, depending on the program and accommodations chosen.

Delaware Museum of Natural History

PO Box 3937
Wilmington, DE 19807

302-658-9111

The museum offers a bird identification workshop in February and March, and a hawk workshop in September and October. These are intensive workshops for intermediate birders.

Costs are about $40.

Denver Museum of Natural History

2001 Colorado Boulevard
Denver, CO 80205

303-370-6307

This museum offers many 1- to 3-day workshops on the natural history of the Front Range of the Rocky Mountains. Sections cover geology, ornithology, and other natural history topics.

Length and cost vary by programs and are available in seasonal announcements.

Field Museum of Natural History
Roosevelt Road and Lake Shore Drive
Chicago, IL 60605-2496

312-922-9410

A wide variety of local and international travel programs and field seminars are offered by the Field Museum. Write for a copy of their most recent offerings for more information about costs, topics, and length.

The High Desert Museum
59800 South Highway 97
Bend, OR 97702

503-382-4754

A mother and her two children enjoy a hands-on analysis of an Oregon salt marsh. (*Photo courtesy of The High Desert Museum*)

This museum offers 2 types of programs. The first is a series of 3- to 10-day field excursions to places such as Death Valley, the Great Basin, the Snake River Birds-of-Prey Area, Alaska's coastal wilderness, and the Cascades. The second is a series of 1-day workshops on a variety of natural history subjects on the high desert country. There is also a 5-day field ornithology course offered most summers. College credit is offered for the field ornithology course through Portland State University.

The cost ranges from free participation to $1,200.

Institute of Ecosystem Studies
The New York Botanical Garden
Mary Flagler Arboretum
Box AB
Millbrook, NY 12545

914-677-5358

The institute offers a wide range of continuing education programs, including a certificate program in landscape design and gardening; workshops that promote an ecological approach to horticulture, landscape design, land management, land use planning, and similar projects; courses in natural science illustration; and ecological excursions to various sites in New York.

Costs are very reasonable.

Natural History Museum of Los Angeles County
Adult Programs Coordinator
900 Exposition Boulevard
Los Angeles, CA 90007

213-744-3534
FAX 213-746-2999

This museum offers lectures, adult classes and workshops, field trips, and children's programs, all of which are connected with the natural history of Los Angeles County or exhibits at the museum.

Recent offerings have included Watercolor in the Santa Monica Mountains, Birding at the Nature Conservancy's Kern River Preserve, Under the Sea—A Snorkeling Excursion to Catalina Island, and Grand Family Hike and Native Plant Feast.

These are all 1-day events and cost between $25 and $100.

The Nature Place
Colorado Outdoor Education Center
Florissant, CO 80816

719-748-3475
719-748-3341

This facility was especially designed to meet the needs of adult educational organizations and also offers some programs for individuals.

The Nature Place can tailor natural history programs to the specific needs of groups, and these can range from the overview Natural History Program to programs featuring geology, paleontology, botany, history, or wildlife photography. All courses and programs are taught by trained naturalists.

Some programs that are family and individual oriented are the 7- day special events held the last week in December. Other 1-week programs scattered throughout the year feature outdoor recreation adventures, wildflower excursions, and geological explorations.

The Nature Place is located 35 miles west of Colorado Springs on 6,000 acres of beautiful mountain land. The National Park Service has designated the center as a National Environmental Study Area.

There are 32 deluxe studio apartments at the center, and there is a large dining room that serves meals.

Rates are $80 to $140 per day.

Orange County Marine Institute
PO Box 68
Dana Point, CA 92629

714-496-2274
714-831-3850
FAX 714-248-5557

This private, nonprofit organization offers field trips and programs to help increase public awareness of the marine environment and does so at several separate facilities. These are the 130-foot-tall ship *Pilgrim* (which is a replica of the ship Richard Henry Dana sailed on), the 65-foot research vessel *Sum Fun*, 2 fully equipped teaching laboratories, the Dana Point Marine Life Refuge, the *Ocean in Motion* traveling marine van, and the 160-acre Chaparral to Ocean Residential Science School.

Most of their programs focus on school groups, but they offer programs open to all during most of the year.

Resource Institute
6532 Phinney Avenue North, Building B
Seattle, WA 98103
206-784-6762

The Resource Institute offers small group natural history seminars at various times during the year aboard the schooner *Crusader*. Each seminar is designed for the needs of the people in the group.

Tours include sailing around the San Juan Archipelago and in the waters of southeast Alaska.

Rio Grande Nature Center
2901 Candelaria NW
Albuquerque, NM 87107
505-344-7240

The center offers many day hikes and programs for those interested in the region around Albuquerque.

San Antonio Museum Association
PO Box 2601
San Antonio, TX 78299-2601
512-226-5544

The association conducts informal education programs for all of San Antonio, including the natural history museum.

San Diego Natural History Museum
Educational Programs
PO Box 1390
San Diego, CA 92112
619-232-3821

What could be more educational (and pleasant) than a walk through the woods?
(*Photo by Bill Evans, courtesy of the San Diego Museum of Natural History*)

The education department offers a series of 1-day and 1-week classes for young people during the summer. These are mostly geared to preschoolers and primary grades, with some requiring parents to attend.

There are also a number of 1-day, guided nature walks in the deserts and mountains to the east of San Diego. These are led by volunteers trained by the museum to teach an appreciation of the native plants and animals of the natural areas of San Diego County.

Classes cost from $15 to $150, and the nature walks are free.

Santa Barbara Zoological Gardens
Education Programs
500 Ninos Drive
Santa Barbara, CA 93103
805-962-5339
FAX 805-962-1673

The zoo offers a series of 1-day educational programs during the year, mostly for elementary-age students, but some involve both adults and children. Each year they also offer a Zoo Camp during July and August and during winter vacation.

The Zoo Camp, which is a day program with 1 overnight in some weeks, can be fit into a vacation to the region.

Programs cost between $25 and $90.

Seaside Nature Center
Cape Henlopen State Park
42 Henlopen Drive
Lewes, Delaware 19958
302-645-6852

This nature center sits on a peninsula with a 4-mile beach. The Great Dune rises 80 feet above the shore and overlooks shoreline, pinelands, and cranberry bogs. This dune is the highest between Cape Hatteras and Cape Cod. Nearby are walking dunes that have been featured in *National Geographic* magazine. Unusual flora and a seabird nesting colony add to the explorative opportunities at the nature center.

At present the center has a salt marsh field studies program that includes an opportunity to seine for sea creatures in the Delaware Bay. New programs are also being developed.

Contact the center for more information about available programs.

Seattle Aquarium
1483 Alaskan Way
Seattle, WA 98101
206-386-4329

The aquarium offers many 1- and 2-day programs for children and adults throughout the year that concentrate on the Puget Sound area, and a week-long workshop on Puget Sound Ecology for adults. College credits are available for the workshop.

Shirley Heinze Environmental Fund
PO Box 114
Beverly Shores, IN 46301
219-879-4725

This nonprofit land trust was founded in 1981 to maintain, expand, and protect unspoiled dunelands in the Indiana Dunes. It offers spring and fall educational hikes that are open to all and occasional member hikes to places of special interest.

Three Circles Center for Multicultural Environmental Education
410 B Johnson Street
Sausalito, CA 94965
415-331-4540

Three Circles Center attempts to introduce, encourage, and cultivate multicultural perspectives and values in environmental and outdoor education, recreation, and interpretation. Teachers and others who work with children in environmental education are trained how to address ethnically and culturally diverse populations.

University of Kansas
Museum of Natural History
Lawrence, KS 66045-2454

913-864-4173

Year-round weekend workshops for children and adults, and week-long summer workshops for young people are both offered by the museum.

Vermont Institute of Natural Science
PO Box 86
Woodstock, VT 05091

802-457-2779

VINS offers many programs for children and adults, including workshops for teachers and interested adults that can be taken for graduate credit. It also houses the Vermont Raptor Center, which is a living museum with 26 species of owls, hawks, and eagles that are native to Vermont.

The Wetlands Institute
Stone Harbor Boulevard
Stone Harbor, NJ 08247

609-368-1211

The Wetlands Institute is a private nonprofit environmental research center dedicated to the wise use of the Atlantic coastal region's natural resources.

It offers field study programs and wildlife photography workshops throughout the year.

Whitefish Point Bird Observatory

Highway Contract 48, Box 115
Paradise, MI 49768

906-492-3596

Whitefish Point Bird Observatory is a research and educational facility affiliated with the Michigan Audubon Society. In addition to its basic mission of documenting the distribution and abundance of birds in the Great Lakes region, the observatory conducts a comprehensive educational program that includes bird walks and talks throughout the year, as well as extensive identification workshops. These all require preregistration and are limited to 10 people.

The observatory also arranges birding trips to various sites in the U.S. and Mexico.

The cost for the workshops is $50. Trips range from $400 to $800 for 6 to 8 days.

Field Institutes and
Natural History Associations

One of the best ways to study the natural history of an area is to locate field institutes or natural history associations in the region and attend one or more of their formal programs. Many of these organizations are affiliated with a national or state park, but others are freestanding, nonprofit educational institutions that teach natural history to adults and children outside in nature.

Many of these institutes are affiliated with local colleges or universities so that participants can receive college credit for attending their courses, but those that don't can often assist you if you wish to locate a college that will offer you credit.

Many of the field institutes included in this section are at least loosely connected with state and national parks, but they are not the only educational activities that take place in these settings. Almost every large state and national park in the U.S. and Canada, and in many other countries, has ongoing naturalists' programs that include hikes, campfires, and other naturalists' activities that all visitors can enjoy. These programs give you a good introduction to the natural history of the park with little investment of time or money, but they do not delve as deeply into the study of the region as programs offered by field institutes.

Adirondack Park Visitor Centers

PO Box 3000
Paul Smiths, NY 12970

518-327-3000

The 2 visitor centers in the Adirondack State Park (the largest park, state or national, in the continental U.S.) offer a variety of workshops and seminars each year. Most of these are oriented to school-age youth, but each summer there is an institute on some environmental topic for teachers that is offered for credit.

Contact the center headquarters for more information about current workshops.

Big Bend Natural History Association

PO Box 68
Big Bend National Park, TX 79834

915-477-2236

Seminars offered by this association center around Big Bend National Park, Big Bend Ranch State Natural Area, and Lake Amistad National Recreation Area in southwest Texas. The sessions generally have between 5 and 15 participants and vary from those that involve very little or no hiking to those with day hikes of 4 to 10 hours with elevation gains or losses of 100 to 1,500 feet.

Photography, plant and wildlife, reading and writing about nature, float trips, geology, waterpainting, history, and archaeology are all subjects covered in the seminars. These are taught by instructors who have lived and worked in the region for years, and many have published works in their field of study.

The seminars last from 1 to 5 days and cost between $15 and $420. Participants generally camp in the parks during their stay.

Canyonlands Field Institute

PO Box 68
Moab, UT 84532
801-259-7750

The consummate "Wilderness U." classroom: an alpine meadow and pond. (*Photo courtesy of the Canyonlands Field Institute*)

This educational, nonprofit organization offers programs that promote understanding and appreciation of the Colorado Plateau, with the hope that this increased awareness will lead to informed personal action on issues affecting the plateau's future.

Canyonlands Field Institute offers a variety of programs that range from half-day walks and full-day trips to photography workshops, backpack excursions, multiday seminars, and special EDventure trips to Baja California and Belize. All but the EDventure trips focus on the natural history of the beautiful Canyon-lands area of southeastern Utah.

These programs are taught by trained naturalists—both permanent staff and guest instructors—and most participants stay in a rustic field camp.

The courses and seminars last from 1 to 5 days and cost between $90 and $700. College credit is available for most seminars.

Chet Ager Nature Center

Lincoln Parks and Recreation Department
2740 A Street
Lincoln, NE 68502
402-471-7895

This small nature center offers a number of 1- and 2-day workshops that focus on the prairies of Nebraska. It also offers a 2-week summer workshop on the natural history of the Lincoln region that can be taken for credit.

Cloud Ridge Naturalists

8297 Overland Road
Ward, CO 80481
303-459-3248

The nesting ecology of flammulated owls
means more to a student who holds
a chick in her hands.
(*Photo by Audrey D. Benedict,
courtesy of Cloud Ridge Naturalists*)

Cloud Ridge Naturalists began leading groups to special places in the West in 1979 and has provided natural history education to over

2,000 participants since. The field seminars given by the organization have included a wide variety of natural history programs: geology of the Scottsbluff National Monument area, natural history of the Yampa and Green rivers, photography of the Colorado grouse, the forest ecology of Ponderosa pines and goshawks, birds in high places, and much more. They are led by highly trained professionals, many of whom have their Ph.D.'s.

Two naturalist photographers come face-to-face with stunning subject matter: the stark shapes of sand dunes. (*Photo by Audrey D. Benedict, courtesy of Cloud Ridge Naturalists*)

Seminars last from 2 to 10 days, cost between $50 and $675 ($2,900 for a 10-day trip to Alaska and Canada) and are limited to 15 to 20 participants. Some seminars involve strenuous hikes of over 6 miles per day over rugged terrain, while others are suitable for families with children over the age of 9.

Crow Canyon Archaeological Center

23390 County Road K
Cortez, CO 81321

303-565-8975
FAX 303-565-4859

Workshop participants grovel through a garden to study ancient agricultural methods of the Southwest. (*Photo courtesy of the Crow Canyon Archaeological Center*)

Crow Canyon was formed in 1984 as a nonprofit organization dedicated to archaeological research and education. A considerable portion of its program, though, is devoted to environmental archaeology and the study of Southwest ecology. The campus lies on the edge of a region the earliest Spanish explorers called the Great Sage Plain. Even before the Spanish came, however, Puebloan farmers tilled these fertile plateaus and built large stone pueblos on the mesatops.

All course work here is conducted as part of ongoing research projects where participants join with noted researchers in their field activities. Most courses are for 7 days and cost $750. Less expensive weekend courses are also available.

Participants stay in comfortable log hogans on a pinyon- and juniper-covered hillside above the Crow Canyon Lodge, and 3 meals a day are provided.

Eagle Awareness Program
Lake Guntersville State Park
Star Route 63, Box 224
Guntersville, AL 35976-9126

205-582-2061
800-ALA-PARK

Bald eagles were once native inhabitants of Alabama, but their habitat was so destroyed by human intervention that they no longer visited the region by the 1950s. Through the concerted effort of a number of agencies, the bald eagle has returned to the state and is now a regular visitor to Lake Guntersville State Park.

The park offers special weekend and midweek programs during January where participants observe and study the eagle in its natural setting.

The weekend programs are for 2 nights and 2 days and cost from $95 to $115, including room and board. The midweek program is for 2 days and 1 night and costs $39, including room.

Eagle Hill Wildlife Research Station
Steuben, ME 04680

718-622-0452 (before April 1)
207-546-2821 (after April 1)

This is an independent nonprofit organization that conducts research and advanced educational programs in natural history. It is located on the forested summit of 235-foot-high Eagle Hill on the edge of the Atlantic Ocean and overlooks the coast of Maine from Acadia National Park to Petit Manan National Wildlife Refuge.

Intensive week-long seminars are offered primarily for advanced adults and professionals who wish to study specific natural history topics. Some undergraduate students study here, but they are in the minority. Serious amateur naturalists are welcome to study beside university professors, professional field biologists, and teachers.

Participants may earn 2 to 6 graduate or undergraduate credits from the University of Maine. Two units are given for attending the week-long seminar, and up to 4 additional units can be earned by completing a special project after the seminar.

Courses are taught by leading national authorities in various fields of natural history. These include forest entomology, ecological zoogeography, lichens, glacial geology, botany, spiders, marine invertebrates, field ethnobotany, mycology, peatland ecology, and natural history illustration.

The seminars cost $175, plus $30 for registration for 2 units of credit. Additional units include further expense. Most participants live and eat on-site. Housing costs from $75 to $150 per person, but tent sites are free. All meals are covered by $150, and other options are available.

Guests and family members are welcome as nonparticipants if there is space available to house them.

Various scholarships and stipends are available.

Four Corners School of Outdoor Education

East Route
Monticello, UT 84535

801-587-2859
800-525-4456

This nonprofit educational foundation offers courses and workshops on the natural history of the Four Corners Region and the Colorado Plateau. Courses are offered between February and November, generally last from 1 to 2 weeks, and cost between $275 and $1,400. College credit is offered for some courses and workshops.

The Glacier Institute

PO Box 1457B
Kalispell, MT 59903

406-888-5215 (June 15 to August 15)
406-756-3911 (rest of the year)

A backpacking expedition devotes itself to understanding the fragile alpine ecosystem of the High Rockies. (*Photo courtesy of the Glacier Institute*)

This institute, which was established in 1983, provides field classes within the Glacier Park ecosystem during the summer season. The classes examine Glacier's cultural and natural resources and increase participants' awareness of resource issues and research efforts. They also help to increase the appreciation of Glacier's aesthetic qualities through art, photography, and writing programs.

All classes are taught by professionals who have a special relationship with the park and who wish to share their interests in natural science, art, photography, history, and education.

Special 1- and 2-day exploration classes encourage individuals and families to learn about the many wonders of Glacier National Park. Three-day field seminars provide more intense instruction for participants who want more in-depth information. No college credit is offered for the exploration courses, but all of the field seminars are offered for lower-division credit through Flathead Valley Community College or upper-division credit through the University of Montana.

The exploration classes cost between $20 and $100, and the field seminars between $100 and $225.

Seminar participants can stay in rustic cabins at the Glacier Institute facility, in nearby campgrounds, or in motels in West Glacier. Meals can be prepared at the kitchen at the institute or purchased in nearby restaurants.

Great Smoky Mountains Institute at Tremont

Great Smoky Mountains National Park
Townsend, TN 37882

615-448-6709

This institute offers programs for school and university students, youth groups, Elderhostel members, and individuals. Program offerings can be tailored to meet the needs of specific groups.

The institute is located in Walker Valley on the middle prong of Little River near Townsend, Tennessee, in the heart of the Great Smoky Mountains National Park. As part of the Great Smoky Mountains Natural History Association, operated in conjunction with the National Park Service, the mission of the institute is to enhance the understanding and enjoyment of the park by visitors and institute participants.

Special programs such as weekend workshops and Elderhostel courses are held year-round, and summer programs are offered for all ages through discovery camps, wilderness adventure camps, adult and family programs, and teacher-training weeks. All sessions are based at the institute's facilities, which include a modern 4-section dormitory that can house up to 125 people, an activity center, kitchen, dining hall, meeting rooms, classrooms, and an outdoor pavilion with a covered campfire area.

Classes in photography, flyfishing, ecological spirituality, Appalachian crafts, Native American life, backpacking, environmental education, special weekends for high-school students, and similar activities are offered in 2- to 5-day sessions and cost between $50 and $650.

Graduate credits are available for some courses.

The International Wolf Center
1900 East Camp Street
Ely, MN 55731
218-365-7217
800-475-6666

A workshop participant meets a wolf—up close and personal.
(*Photo by Monty Sloan, courtesy of Wolf Park*)

The center attempts to educate people of all ages in all walks of life about the timber wolf (*Canis lupus lycaon*). It offers workshops throughout the year entitled The Wolf: Its World —Its Ways where participants learn wolf ecology from professional biologists and naturalists, use the latest technologies to track wolves, and watch wolf and prey demonstrations.

Credit for these workshops can be arranged through the University of Minnesota, Duluth Community College, or Vermillion Community College. For costs and dates of workshops, contact the center.

This center also offers 2 active natural study sessions. Wolf Weekends encourage you to study the life of the wolf through field excursions, demonstrations of research techniques, and group discussions. Week-long wolf-research expeditions have you spend a week in wolf country radio-tracking wolves through the forests of northern Minnesota.

College credit is available for both sections, and the cost is $270 for the weekends and $580 for the week-long sessions.

Kentucky Department of Parks

Division of Recreation
Capital Plaza Tower
500 Mero Street, 11th Floor
Frankfort, Kentucky 40601-1974
502-564-2172
800-255-PARK

Below the Chained Rocks in Kentucky lies the varied plant community of the Cumberland Plateau. (*Photo courtesy of the Kentucky Department of Parks*)

The Kentucky Department of Parks offers a number of 1- to 5-day natural history workshops throughout the year. These are held in different locations, and information about what is currently being offered can be obtained by calling the above numbers. In 1991 a few of the workshops offered were at Kenlake State Resort Park (A Visit With the Eagles), Pine Mountain State Resort Park (Spring Astronomy Weekend), Natural Bridge State Resort Park (Nature Photography Workshop), and Cumberland Falls State Resort Park

(Insect Lives). The latter was a 3-day course on insect diversity where participants observed, collected, and identified insects and the plants they feed and live on. Although this was not a technical course, it was taught by a highly qualified instructor who led lectures and field trips.

Courses generally cost around $25 and last from 1 to 3 days. For information about college credit, contact the parks department.

Keystone Science School
Box 606
Keystone, CO 80435
303-468-5824
FAX 303-262-0152

The main purpose of this school is to provide outdoor education experiences to students in grades K through 12 and their classroom teachers. Additional programs include adult workshops on Project WILD, Elderhostel programs, Mountain Speaker series, and other advanced workshops that are offered for continuing education credit through the Colorado School of Mines.

Marin Discoveries
11 First Street
Corte Madera, CA 94925
415-927-0410

Marin Discoveries was established in 1974 as an independent, nonprofit organization to introduce the people of the San Francisco Bay area to educational and recreational outdoor experiences. They now offer over 700 programs annually to adults, families, and special populations such as the disabled. The programs are designed to provide instruction on low-impact outdoor activities that lead to a better understanding and appreciation of our natural resources.

All courses and trips are led by experienced naturalists, many of whom have written books and articles in their areas of expertise.

The institute offers adventure-travel tours to Baja California, New Zealand, and Alaska; canoe trips on the Sacramento and Colorado rivers; cruises on the San Francisco Bay and the Pacific Ocean; day and night hikes in the San Francisco Bay region; rock-climbing and photography outings; family outings; and week-long trips to various sites in California and the Southwest.

Costs for individual programs range from $25 to $2,300, and college credit can be received for some programs. If you need the credits, ask for this information before you register.

Marine Sciences Under Sail
School of Environmental Education
PO Box 3994
Hollywood, FL 33023
305-983-7015

Marine Sciences Under Sail offers study cruises for adults, families, and groups of students. These cruises can vary in length from 1 day to 2 weeks, and participants learn about the sea while sailing on it. The programs provide education about the life and history of the sea around Florida, and the areas of study include mangrove islands, barrier islands, shallow seas, coral reefs, open ocean, and the Florida peninsula.

The programs vary considerably, and prices vary greatly. To learn about current offerings contact the school.

Newfound Harbor Marine Institute
Route 3, Box 170
Big Pine Key, FL 33043
305-872-2331

This institute offers many short workshops and seminars that teach about ecology, marine science, biology, and similar subjects in the outdoors. Participants study along trails, on beaches, and among underwater reefs.

North Cascades Institute
2105 Highway 20
Sedro Woolley, WA 98284
206-856-5700

The North Cascades Institute provides innovative programs that put people in touch with the natural world, with an emphasis on quality learning in an enjoyable and adventurous context. Classes are kept small and informal as they focus on depth and intimacy of experience. Programs include over 60 field seminars that take place throughout the North Cascades, ranging from the Fraser River in British Columbia to the Snoqualmie Pass, and from the islands of the Puget Sound to the Columbia Basin.

In addition to the above field seminars, the institute offers training workshops for teachers, summer camps for children, and Elderhostel programs.

Most seminars can be taken for college credit through Western Washington University. The seminars are from 2 to 5 days in length and cost between $80 and $300, plus additional cost for college credits.

Olympic Park Institute
HC 62 Box 9T
Port Angeles, WA 98362
206-928-3720
FAX 206-928-3046

The Olympic Park Institute is a private, nonprofit educational organization that provides environmental learning experiences that emphasize the need for sustaining a balance between prudent use and thoughtful preservation of our natural resources. OPI is 1 of 3 campuses of the Yosemite National Institutes, which have served over 250,000 participants since 1971.

Its programs are based at Rosemary Inn, a historic inn at Lake Crescent on the Olympic Peninsula, and feature the diversity of natural resources found in the Olympic Region, particularly those in Olympic National Park. They are taught by staff trained in experiential learning who hold degrees in natural/earth science, education, or a related field.

Courses vary in length from 1 to 5 days and cost from $50 to $200, most including meals and lodging. A 5-day Elderhostel program is offered in coordination with Elderhostel, International in Boston, Massachusetts (see Elderhostel listing for further information).

College credit can be arranged for some seminars.

For a more detailed description and history of the Olympic Park Institute, see "Olympic Wilderness Classroom" in the Vignettes section.

Pacific Northwest Field Seminars
83 South King Street, Suite 212
Seattle, WA 98104
206-553-2636

Pacific Northwest Field Seminars is sponsored by the Northwest Interpretive Association in cooperation with the National Park Service, U.S. Forest Service, and other state and federal agencies in Washington and Oregon. The collaboration is designed to enhance an individual's knowledge and enjoyment of the natural resources of the region.

Glaciers, ecology, geology, volcanoes, nature photography, nature writing, wild horse management, and bats and caves are just some of the wide-ranging subjects taught by the naturalist instructors of the institute throughout the Northwest. Classes are all held in the field, and participants must furnish their own transportation, food, and lodging except for a very few exceptions. Most are for adults only, but some are open to families.

Classes last from 2 to 5 days and cost between $25 and $125. Many of the classes can be taken for college credit.

Patuxent Wildlife Research Center
Laurel, MD 20708
301-498-0331

Until recently Patuxent concentrated almost exclusively on high-quality research on wildlife in the U.S. This research center was established in 1939 and has grown to be the largest wildlife research center of its kind in the world.

In the past several years they have expanded their public education facilities and now offer a number of educational options. A new $15 million National Wildlife Visitor Center is being constructed as this guide is being written. After completion, tours of the facility will be conducted, and workshops will be offered for teachers, professional wildlife workers, and interested amateurs.

For more information about these new programs, most of which will become available after the visitor center opens in 1993, contact the center at the above number.

Pocono Environmental Education Center
RD 2, Box 1010
Dingman's Ferry, PA 18328
717-828-2319

This organization is the largest residential center for education about the environment in the Western Hemisphere, and it is located along the eastern escarpment of the Pocono Plateau in the Delaware Water Gap National Recreation Area.

Activities include outdoor adventure weekends, family camps and holiday weekends, bird-watching weekends, science workshops, nature study weekends, and environmental issues workshops.

Pennsylvania State University also generally offers a 1-week field studies class each summer. The field studies class is given for credit, and continuing education in-service credit is given for most other offerings. Contact the center for more information about credits.

Most programs are for 3 days and 2 nights (although the family camps are 5 days, Monday through Friday), and the costs are from $70 to $115.

Point Reyes Field Seminars

Point Reyes National Seashore Association
Bear Valley Road
Point Reyes Station, CA 94956
415-663-1200

The field seminar program at Point Reyes offers courses in natural history, photography, environmental education, and the arts, all taught by professionals with exceptional credentials. All courses are conducted on the beautiful Point Reyes Peninsula, which juts out into the Pacific Ocean some 50 miles north of San Francisco.

Courses run from 1 to 5 days in length, cost between $10 and $800, and can be taken for credit through Dominican College of San Rafael. Dormitory accommodations for the longer seminars are offered at either the Clem Miller Environmental Education Center or the Chimney Rock Lifeboat Station.

Redwood Field Seminars

Redwood National Park
111 Second Street
Crescent City, CA 95531
707-464-6101

Redwood Field Seminars offers in-depth outdoor study in Redwood National Park in the extreme northwestern corner of California between April and September. In these seminars you can explore redwood country with a backpack, study the elephant seal and black bear habitats, and touch the sticky tentacles of a sea anemone. All seminars are taught by trained naturalists.

While most of the classes are for adults, children who are comfortable in a class with adults are welcome, and several sessions are offered especially for families each year.

Seminars last from 1 to 3 days, cost $15 to $75, and can be taken for credit through Humboldt State University.

Most of the seminars are held at the Redwood Information Center in Orick, near Prairie Creek Redwoods State Park. Camping is available there, but reservations are highly recommended.

Rocky Mountain Seminars
Rocky Mountain Natural History Association
Rocky Mountain National Park
Estes Park, CO 80517
303-586-2371, ext. 258

The Rocky Mountain Seminars, established in 1961, call themselves A University Without Walls. Their campus extends over the 417 square miles of montane meadows and alpine tundra designated as the Rocky Mountain National Park. Seminars are highlighted by extensive field trips to areas within the park and are taught by instructors familiar with the many features found there. There are also a group of seminars that fall under the umbric of Art in the Park weeks.

Most seminars require hiking, and high altitudes and variable weather conditions add an element of rigor. Participants should be in good health and ready to adapt to the whims of Rocky Mountain summer weather.

Most participants camp near the seminars, and there are rustic accommodations at the Hidden Valley Ski Lodge and Camp Kawuneeche for sessions held there.

Classes are for 1 day, a weekend, or a week, are small in size, and can be taken for credit through the University of Northern Colorado or Colorado State University. They cost between $50 and $150. Special extended natural history tours are also offered each year. Ptarmigan at Guanella Pass, The Migration of the Sandhill Cranes, Colorado Grouse: Blue, Sharp-tailed, and Sage, and Canyonlands Autumn Tour are a few examples.

Santa Cruz Mountains Natural History Association

525 North Big Trees Park Road
Felton, CA 95018

408-335-3174

In 1985 the Santa Cruz Mountains Natural History Association began their annual Old Ways: The World of the California Indian seminar series. This is a living history experience in Native American culture taught through seminars that are designed to provide participants with hands-on activities that take them back in time to share the world of the early California Indians.

Seminars offered include Tracking and Nature Observation, Native Uses of Plants, and The Total Tule, plus others on native arts and crafts activities.

The seminars are generally held in the fall, are from 1 to 3 days in length, cost about $125, and can be taken for credit through San Jose State University.

Instructors for these seminars are either Native Americans or people who have been involved with Native American Studies for many years.

The Schoolship

The Inland Seas Education Association
104 South Union Street, Suite 202
PO Box 4223
Traverse City, MI 49685-4223

616-941-5577

The Schoolship operates aboard the 106-foot gaff topsail schooner *The Malabar*, and it is a half-day educational experience that involves participants in the history, culture, and ecology of the Great Lakes. While the main focus of this program is to accommodate students and their classroom teachers during the school year, it does offer outings for adults for 4 weeks between mid-May and mid-June and for 3 weeks in September.

Schoolship students discuss the history and ecology of the Great Lakes aboard the 106-foot schooner *The Malabar*. (*Photo by John Elder, courtesy of the Inland Seas Education Association*)

Teton Science School

PO Box 8
Kelly, WY 83011

307-733-4765

This school operates a year-round program at a former dude ranch 20 miles northeast of Jackson, Wyoming, in the Grand Teton National Park. It provides students with an experiential natural science education within the Greater Yellowstone ecosystem, and its goal is to make all students ecologically literate. It teaches all age groups year-round. In 1990 over 2,800 students attended programs.

The campus of 25 log buildings is surrounded by spectacular mountains, aspen forests, open grasslands, and a rich wildlife population. Elk, moose, bison, coyote, and antelope are frequently seen on campus.

Courses are available for all students between 8 years of age and senior citizens, both in residential and nonresidential programs. Courses take students into the field for a hands-on approach to natural science learning that stresses the basic concepts of ecology and specific aspects of the greater Yellowstone ecosystem.

The permanent staff is comprised of professional natural science teachers, and experts in many natural science fields serve as guest faculty.

Programs include junior high field ecology, high-school field natural history and field ecology, college courses in environment and ecology, young naturalist nonresident programs, adult resident programs such as teacher workshops, wilderness EMT training, Elderhostel, and a wide variety of nonresidential adult seminars. College credit can be obtained for almost all courses for adults.

Courses are from 1 day to 6 weeks in length and cost between $50 and $1800.

Budding naturalists take notes as they observe hoofed mammals in the high country of Wyoming. (*Photo by Kirk Wilson, courtesy of Teton Science School*)

Trees for Tomorrow Natural Resources Education Center

611 Sheridan Street
PO Box 609
Eagle River, WI 54521

715-479-6456

This was the first natural resources education center in the U.S., according to its director, and it offers year-round, on-site resource education programs at its 40-acre wooded campus in the Wisconsin north woods. It offers programs and workshops for students from elementary through high school, and about two- thirds of the participants of workshops at the center are students and their teachers.

Adult programs are also offered. The University of Wisconsin, Superior, offers 1- and 2-week-long courses at the center each summer for credit. These cost between $250 and $450.

The Wilderness Institute

28118 Agoura Road
Agoura Hills, CA 91301

818-991-7327

The Wilderness Institute was created by a former National Park Service employee to offer people who love the outdoors a way to experience the beauty and serenity of the wilderness in the Santa Monica Mountains National Recreation Area, which covers a large segment of the Santa Monica Mountains to the northwest of Los Angeles.

The institute helps program participants experience nature in new ways, and brings together people who have a common interest in exploration, adventure, and a connection with the earth.

All institute instructors are experienced outdoor professionals. They provide participants with instruction in wilderness skills and natural and cultural history.

Special programs are available for families, youth, men or women only, and for people with disabilities.

Courses cover the cultural and natural history of the Santa Monica Mountains and surrounding area, are offered year round, last from 1 to 7 days, and cost from nothing to $300.

The Yellowstone Institute
PO Box 117
Yellowstone National Park, WY 82190
307-344-7381, ext. 2349

Field students learn how to identify wild animal tracks.
(*Photo by Gene Ball, courtesy of the Yellowstone Institute*)

The institute is housed at the old Buffalo Ranch overlooking the beautiful Lamar Valley in Yellowstone National Park, where bison, deer, bighorn sheep, and other wildlife are abundant. The buildings at the institute include a large log structure that is used for a community kitchen and classrooms, and simple, rustic cabins where participants sleep.

Classes are purposefully kept between 10 and 14 students so that everyone can have personal and individualized contact with the seminar or class leader. Participants explore everything from wildflowers to grizzly bear ecology, to geysers and mudpots, to nature photography, to early human history in Yellowstone, to flyfishing and how trout live. There are also plenty of classes for bird- watchers.

Many classes concentrate on the area around the institute campus, but others head into the backcountry, each with a specific theme.

Most classes are for adults, but there are at least a half-dozen classes that are designed specifically for families.

About 20 of the 70 courses offered in 1991 were offered for college credit.

Seminars are from 3 to 5 days long and cost between $75 and $500.

Yosemite Field Seminars

PO Box 230
El Portal, CA 95318

209-379-2646

This program, 1 of 3 programs operated by the Yosemite National Institutes, has offered a wide variety of outdoor classes and back-

Outdoor education in the style and surroundings of Yosemite National Park. (*Photo courtesy of the Yosemite Association*)

trips in and around Yosemite Valley since 1973. They are led by well-qualified instructors.

Courses are geared to different levels of experience, from introductory explorations to specialized academic field courses and surveys. Some can be taken for college credit.

All programs involve hiking, with some more strenuous than others.

Most summer programs provide tent campsites shared by participants. Those conducted at the Crane Flat campus provide rustic dormitory accommodations and family-style meals.

Programs last from 2 to 12 days and cost between $45 and $295.

Clubs and
National Associations

There are many membership organizations and clubs throughout the U.S. and Canada whose primary purpose is to provide education about nature to their members. This education can be through formal programs such as regularly scheduled seminars, tours and trips led by trained naturalists, camps of various types where participants learn about the natural history of the region, or research projects. Many of these organizations, such as the Audubon Society and the National Wildlife Federation, have broad-based programs that help educate the public about a wide range of natural history topics. Others, such as Desert Survivors, have a very narrow focus and attract members with specific interests.

Whatever your interests may be, there should be some club or organization listed below that covers them. If there isn't, you may want to look at some of the books listed in the bibliography to locate one, or if your interests are very narrow, say, mushrooms, you may want to contact the local chapter of the Mycological Society (or whatever group covers your interest areas) where you are planning to vacation for information about their meetings and workshops.

Adirondack Mountain Club
PO Box 867
Lake Placid, NY 12946
518-523-3441

Many parks offer separate workshops for parents and children so each member of the family can learn more about nature.
(*Photo courtesy of Adirondack State Park*)

The Adirondack Mountain Club was established in 1922 and now has more than 19,000 members. The club is dedicated to the enjoyment and protection of the wildlands of New York, and it does this with recreational and educational opportunities that are available through the club's lodges, facilities, and programs.

The Adirondacks are the largest wilderness area in the eastern U.S., and the workshops and field study programs offered by the club use the forests, mountains, wetlands, and lakes of the region as an outdoor classroom where participants can learn firsthand about the flora and fauna of the local terrain.

The field seminars and workshops are offered year-round at Adirondack Lodge, Johns Brook Lodge, club headquarters, and throughout the Adirondack State Park.

Participants can choose from guided hikes and high peak traverses, wilderness experiences by backpack or canoe, courses in outdoor skills from canoeing to map and compass, and field studies of natural history.

Programs last from 1 to 5 days and cost between $50 and $120. Participants can find room and board at one of the lodges or campgrounds operated by the club or in the state park.

American Cetacean Society

PO Box 2639
San Pedro, CA 90731-0943
213-548-6279
FAX 213-548-6950

This is the oldest whale protection group in the world, and its membership includes scientists and educators, as well as interested laypersons. The group works in the areas of education, research, and conservation to protect whales and dolphins.

As part of its educational program the society offers a number of whale-watching trips each year. These run about 8 to 10 days, cost about $1,500 to $2,000, and explore the waters around Baja California.

American Littoral Society

Highlands, NJ 07732
908-291-0055

A national, nonprofit public-interest organization of professional and amateur naturalists, the American Littoral Society was founded in 1961 by a group of divers, naturalists, and fishermen to encourage a better understanding of aquatic environments and provide a unified voice advocating protection of the delicate fabric of life along the shore.

The littoral zone is the shore of the ocean with its adjacent wetlands, bays, and rivers, and many individuals, from birders to beachcombers, are interested in and use this zone.

The society is an active group that devotes much of its effort and time to outdoor field experiences. Field trips are part of the experience, and the society offers coastal trips of varying duration and cost. Local New Year's Day beach walks; spring and fall oyster dives in the Chesapeake Bay; whale watching off Cape Cod or Montauk; island weekends in Spruce Head, Maine; a week at the Bermuda Biological Station; a birding weekend at Cape May, New Jersey; and hiking the Olympic Peninsula in the state of Washington are just some of the field trips where members study about littoral zones around the U.S.

The trips last from 1 day to over a week and cost between $50 and $1,000. These trips are open to everyone regardless of their expertise as naturalists.

Canyon Explorers Club
1223 Frances Avenue
Fullerton, CA 92631
No phone number available

The basic purpose of the Canyon Explorers Club is to explore remote and exciting places around the world. All trips emphasize the out-of-doors, natural science, and native cultures, and the club strives to operate the trips so that wilderness areas will be preserved and the dignity and integrity of native cultures will be respected.

The club uses only volunteer leaders, and all trips are run on a share-the-cost and share-the-responsibility basis. This helps minimize costs.

Trips vary in difficulty from easy camping-out to strenuous backpacking and technical climbing, last from 1 to 18 days, and cost from nothing to $5,000.

Most members of the club live in Southern California, but others are welcome to join and participate in all club activities.

Chesapeake Bay Foundation
162 Prince George Street
The Church
Annapolis, MD 21401

301-268-8816

This foundation, which was formed as a conservation organization to promote responsible and appropriate management of the resources of Chesapeake Bay, has over 65,000 members and a full-time staff of 90 people.

One function of this staff is to operate field trips for students of all ages. The philosophy of these trips is to 1) keep the students actively involved, 2) get the students on the water and in the field, 3) work closely with teachers and group leaders, and 4) be safe.

The most active part of the educational program is the section devoted to working with public schools, but the foundation offers a number of other activities and trips. Any group of at least 20 people, whether a club, a class, or a family, can arrange for a special field trip. In addition, the foundation offers field trips open to the general public, and in-service courses that can be taken by teachers or other interested adults for 4 units of college credit.

Contact the foundation for the program that most interests you.

Desert Survivors
PO Box 20991
Oakland, CA 94620-0991

415-357-6585

Desert Survivors is a group of people who like to explore the American desert wilderness and are committed to its study and protection. Desert Survivors recognizes that this wilderness will not survive unless those who appreciate it are vigilant and act to preserve it.

To help further this goal the organization offers guided tours to desert areas, mostly in California and Nevada, that are generally 3- or 4-day weekend trips, although a few are longer. These are car-camp trips with hiking, easy backpack trips, and difficult backpack trips.

Many of these trips explore obscure and unknown desert places, which makes them a true learning experience for even seasoned desert travelers.

Most trips focus on the area's geology, botany, wildlife, human history, and prehistory. They are conducted by leaders who have been visiting the desert for 20 years or more with field guides and maps in hand. Participants often come away from the trips saying, "I never knew there was that much out there in the desert."

All trips are a cooperative effort, and everyone shares equally in transportation and food.

Earth Spirit, Inc.
PO Box 261
Orchard Park, NY 14127
716-941-6267

Earth Spirit is a nonprofit membership organization. Its naturalists interpret the stories of field and forest, plant and animal, and offer lessons in the never-ending classroom of nature. They remind participants that living gently with nature is not just something of the past, but a vital lesson for the present.

Earth Spirit offers a variety of outdoor-skill-oriented/nature-based programs for youths and adults. Program topics include earth awareness, field ecology, wildlife studies, historic survival, and living with nature. They also offer a series of 1- day seminars in their year-long Living Naturally series.

Costs vary by program, and 1-day seminars cost from $10 to $50.

The staff also offers 2 courses (Field Ecology and The Ethics of Survival) through the University of Buffalo Department of Social Sciences.

Mono Lake Foundation

PO Box 153
Lee Vining, CA 93541
619-646-6496

The foundation and its sister organization, the Mono Lake Committee, are dedicated to the preservation of the Mono Basin ecosystem through education and research. As part of this, they offer a series of summer and fall weekend-long seminars that introduce participants to the ecology of the basin. Seminars on birds, wildflowers, mammals, and geology of the basin, as well as on the high country to the west, are led by experienced naturalists.

Seminars cost $75, and participants are responsible for their own room and board. There are several nearby campgrounds, but motel rooms are scarce.

Montana Wilderness Association

PO Box 635
Helena, MT 59624
406-443-7350

The Montana Wilderness Association sponsors an annual program of wilderness walks that introduces participants to the wild places of Montana. Each outing is an opportunity to learn about natural and cultural values of the pristine lands of Montana and to study wildlife, plants, habitats, geology, old-growth forests, and resource management issues.

Montana enjoys an abundance of unspoiled mountain lands, rich wildlife populations, and clear-flowing streams—now some of the last preserved territories left in the U.S. They, like so many other unspoiled wilderness areas in the U.S., are in danger of being lost forever. Mining, clear-cut logging, oil and gas development, and motor vehicles threaten as much as two-thirds of the wilderness in the state.

Participants of the 1- to 7-day wilderness walks sponsored by the association will find themselves sharing with others a belief that these areas must be saved for future generations.

All participants provide their own food, transportation to trail-heads, and gear. Association members are volunteer leaders of all walks.

The Mountaineers
300 Third Avenue, West
Seattle, WA 98119

206-284-6310

The Mountaineers was founded in 1906 to explore, study, preserve, and enjoy the natural beauty of the northwestern U.S. Today it is one of the largest conservation outdoor organizations in the country. In addition to hikes and backpacking trips for individuals and families, the club offers a number of naturalists trips and photography outings that last from 1 to 3 days. Contact them for their most recent outings schedule.

National Audubon Society
Ecology Camps and Workshops
613 Riversville Road
Greenwich, CT 06831

203-869-2017

An expedition group studies
the geology of the Southwest while
traipsing through Utah's Paria Canyon.
(*Photo courtesy of the Audubon
Expedition Institute*)

The National Audubon Society has offered camps for adults for over 50 years. The first of these was the Audubon Camp in Maine, which still operates, and this has since been joined by the Audubon Camp in the West, which is located in a glaciated valley 7,500 feet high in Wyoming's Wind River Mountains.

At these camps adults search ponds for whirligig beetles, dredge the ocean floor for starfish, or listen to coyotes call under a moonlit sky. Whatever they do, participants take home a new awareness of how nature works, how all life is interdependent, and how they can protect the natural world.

In addition to the camps, the National Audubon Society offers field study programs and natural history workshops in Florida, Connecticut, the Southwest Canyonlands, Big Bend National Park, Yellowstone, Hawaii, California, and on the Olympic Peninsula. There are special ecology workshops in Connecticut, Florida, southeast Arizona, and Yellowstone.

International ecology workshops are held in Costa Rica, Venezuela, and Trinidad.

The workshops and camps in the U.S. last between 6 and 12 days and cost from $495 to $1,795. The international workshops are for 10 and 12 days and cost from $1,695 to $1,895, which includes international airfare from Miami. College credit is offered for participation in many of the workshops and camps.

The national organization is not the only Audubon group to offer workshops and field study programs. A number of the state and regional chapters also offer them. Following are a few that offer regularly scheduled programs.

For added information about the National Audubon Society summer camps, see "Beneath Sun and Stars, Campers Learn the Tools of Activism" in the Vignettes section.

Audubon Naturalist Society
8940 Jones Mill Road
Chevy Chase, MD 20815
301-652-5964

This chapter of the National Audubon Society offers special summer institutes, summer courses for teachers, family programs, 1-day and extended adult forays, and natural history field studies, many of which are held at Woodend, the chapter's wildlife sanctuary and headquarters.

The natural history field studies are offered for credit through the USDA Graduate School.

Programs are from 1 to 14 days, and most cost between $20 and $100. The extended adult forays cost considerably more, and information about these can be obtained by calling or writing the chapter.

Audubon Society of New Hampshire
PO Box 528-B
Concord, NH 03302-0516
603-224-9909
FAX 603-226-0902

This chapter offers a number of environmental education institutes and workshops for teachers throughout the year. It also offers a series of courses, workshops, field trips, and special events that are of interest to adults. Some of these are given for credit.

Programs are from 1 to 10 days and cost between $10 and $1,700.

Audubon Society of Rhode Island
12 Sanderson Road
Smithfield, RI 02917-2606
401-231-6444

This chapter offers a number of 1-day walks and workshops at its sanctuaries, a course in Teaching Rhode Island Ecology, a Block Island Birding Weekend, and a camp for parents and children at the Caratunk Wildlife Refuge each summer.

Maine Audubon Society

Gilsland Farm
118 U.S. Route 1
Falmouth, ME 04105

207-781-2330

The primary adult educational activities provided by this chapter take place at its Scarborough Marsh Nature Center, where numerous 1-day activities are scheduled throughout the year. In addition to its adult activities, the chapter also operates the Mast Landing Nature Day Camp for children.

Massachusetts Audubon Society

South Great Road
Lincoln, MA 01773

617-259-9500

This chapter has 18 sanctuaries where a variety of natural history programs are offered, as well as nature day camps for children. The chapter also offers a number of natural history travel expeditions to such locales as Death Valley, Alaska, British Columbia, and Africa. These are offered through the Audubon Travel Alliance, an affiliation of independent Audubon Societies that works to promote natural history travel.

New Jersey Audubon Society

790 Ewing Avenue
PO Box 125
Franklin Lakes, NJ 07417

201-891-2185

This chapter has a strong birding program and offers many 1- to 3-day bird trips in the New Jersey region. It also offers other natural history walks and workshops at its 5 sanctuaries.

Seattle Audubon

8028 35th Avenue, NE
Seattle, WA 98115

No phone number available

Seattle Audubon offers field courses in birding throughout the year.

Tucson Audubon Society

300 East University Boulevard, #120
Tucson, AZ 85705

602-629-0757 (prefers written queries)

For years 60 participants have gathered at the Institute of Desert Ecology each spring to explore the varied ecosystems of the Sonoran Desert. Some of Arizona's foremost natural history authorities teach and guide these participants as they discover hidden ecological treasures of the desert.

Field sessions focus on Sonoran Desert ecosystems rather than classification and identification. Relationships between the plants, wildlife, and the desert environment are the primary concern of the workshops.

The sessions last for 4 days, cost $245, and credit is available through the University of Arizona.

National Wildlife Federation

1400 16th Street, NW
Washington, D.C. 20036-2266

800-245-5484

This is the largest conservation organization in the world, with almost 6 million members. As part of its educational program the federation offers 10- to 20-day guided tours to Africa and Alaska where participants can study nature and wildlife.

For more intensive educational activities, the federation offers conservation summits, wildlife camps, teen adventures, and outdoor education training programs entitled NatureQuest.

Conservation summits offer members unique opportunities to experience some of the nation's most spectacular regions—old-growth forests in the Pacific Northwest, the Colorado Rockies, Yellowstone National Park, Lake Champlain in Vermont, the Monterey Peninsula in California, and the mountains of North Carolina. They offer a varied program with classes, hikes, cruises, ecology field study, and even special programs for teens and youngsters. A program for educators is offered at each summit, and a special educators' summit is offered each summer.

Wildlife Camps and Teen Adventures are 12- to 15-day explorations in the Colorado Rockies or the Black Mountains of North Carolina that provide nature education in a camp setting.

NatureQuest is a certified outdoor education training program for camp directors, nature and science counselors, naturalists, outdoor educators, or adults who are interested in becoming any of these.

You must be a member of the federation to participate in any of these programs. To become a member, call 1-800-432-6564. Basic membership and a bimonthly subscription to *National Wildlife* magazine costs $16.

Some of the programs can be taken for college credit through prior arrangement.

The Nature Conservancy

1815 North Lynn Street
Arlington, VA 22209

703-841-5300

The Nature Conservancy and its over 40 field offices offer a variety of natural history learning experiences for its members. The national office provides a number of natural history travel options, many international, and the field offices offer many 1- to 3-day field study trips. Some, such as the Montana/Wyoming Field Office, also offer week-long field seminars on subjects relating to their region.

For more information about the conservancy, contact them about membership. After you have joined the organization, you can write to the field office that serves the region you are interested in visiting to find out what programs are being offered there.

New England Wildflower Society
Garden in the Woods
Hemenway Road
Framingham, MA 01701
508-877-7630
617-237-4924

The society organizes field trips to unusual ecological and botanical sites to increase the public's understanding and appreciation of native plants and their habitats. In addition, it offers courses in wetland studies, botany, and horticulture.

These activities are generally for 1 day, but some of the courses are for several days spread out over weeks.

The society also sponsors family days and a fall festival where participants can learn about the native plants of New England.

Also offered is a Certificate in Native Plant Studies for those who complete a designed course of study.

Field trips and courses cost between $20 and $150.

A 10-day natural history expedition to Central America is generally arranged for February of each year. This trip costs about $2,500 plus airfare to the country.

North American Wildlife Park Foundation
Battle Ground, IN 47920
317-567-2265
FAX 317-567-2084

This is a nonprofit organization dedicated to research and public education about wolves. Wolf Park, with over 20 wolves in residence, is open to the public from May 1 through November 30 each year, and visitors can learn about the wolves through observation and lectures.

In addition, the foundation offers 2 educational programs for those interested in learning more in-depth information about wolf behavior. The first is a series of 6-day Wolf Behavior seminars. While these are attended by dog trainers and wolf/dog owners, each seminar has a large percentage of participants who are there just to learn about wolves. Each participant personally observes wolf behavior, and then gets extensive hands-on experience working with wolves in a pack situation. There is also special instruction in wolf photography.

The second is a 4-week Ethology Practicum where all participants get extensive experience observing and working directly with wolves, bison, waterfowl, and other free-living species. Proper observation and recording techniques are taught, as well as how to interpret the behavior observed.

The seminars cost $350 and the Ethology Practicum costs $250. Participants stay at a nearby motel or in the dormitory at the park.

Project Ocean Search
The Cousteau Society
930 West 21st Street
Norfolk, VA 23517
804-627-1144

As part of the society's ongoing education program, a sea-land field study program offers expedition experiences each year. Since it is impossible for the society to honor the many requests it receives from people interested in joining the research expeditions undertaken by their ships *Calypso* and *Alcyone*, it has developed Project Ocean Search.

POS provides dramatic, in-depth education that cultivates an appreciation for natural systems and a personal understanding of humankind's relationship with the environment. Participants dive, hike, and talk with expedition crew members, Jean-Michel Cousteau, and lecturers who are experts in their fields.

In the summers of 1990 and 1991 the society offered 2 projects in the Fiji Islands. Traditionally POS takes place on an island removed from the pressures of urban civilization. The philosophy of the program is a belief that a deep understanding of nature comes best from personal experience. Consequently a significant portion of each day is devoted to field activities exploring the natural system.

Daily scuba dives focus on different aspects of natural history, and hikes allow the participants to explore the island with experienced naturalists or to work with biologists to learn research techniques.

Afternoons and evenings are spent with lectures and audiovisual presentations.

The programs are 2 weeks in length and cost about $4,000. This cost covers all program activities, including airfare to the site.

For a personal account of the Project Ocean Search experience, see "Fiji" in the Vignettes section.

Safari Club International
4800 West Gates Pass Road
Tucson, AZ 85745-9645

602-620-1220
FAX 602-622-1205

Safari Club International developed the American Wilderness Leadership School in 1976 to help both students and teachers realize that the wise use of our natural resources is vital to the future of the country. In 1982 the organization purchased the Granite Ranch southeast of Jackson Hole, Wyoming, as the site for the school. The location is within the Gros Ventre Wilderness Area of the Bridger-Teton National Forest and is surrounded by over 8 million acres of public lands.

The curriculum of the school was designed to give maximum exposure to the many considerations affecting natural resource management, resource development and utilization, and planning on community and regional levels.

Outstanding high-school students are selected to attend the program each summer, and teachers and others interested in acquiring outdoor education skills and techniques can get 2 units of university

Students study stream ecology (and while they're at it, learn to cast) in this Safari Club flyfishing course. (*Photo by Don Brown, courtesy of Safari Club International*)

graduate credit from Indiana University for participating in the Wildlife Ecology and Conservation Workshop.

Both high-school students and adults spend 10 days learning about wildlife ecology and conservation through hands-on workshops in the classroom and the field that emphasize a conceptual understanding of natural resource issues. Both also learn the skills and techniques necessary for a safe, enjoyable time in the outdoors.

For a more detailed description of the opportunities offered at the American Wilderness Leadership School, see "The AWLS Experience" in the Vignettes sections.

Wyoming Outdoor Council
201 Main Street
Lander, WY 82520
307-332-7031

The council offers a 5-day workshop for professional and interested amateur naturalists entitled Conservation Biology and Wyoming's Endangered Species at the Grand Teton National Park in August.

The course is for anyone who is interested in the wise management of our natural environment and is led by visiting professionals with outstanding credentials. Participants also complete fieldwork with the staff of the Teton Science School studying threatened and endangered species of the Greater Yellowstone area such as grizzlies, trumpeter swans, black-footed ferrets, whooping cranes, and wolves.

The workshop functions in a nonresidential setting using the Jackson Hole and Grand Teton National Park areas as an outdoor classroom.

Participants can camp in the Gros Ventre Campground. The workshop costs $150, and graduate credit is available from the University of Wyoming for an additional cost.

YMCA of the Rockies

Schlessman Center Executive Offices
Estes Park, CO 80511-2800

303-586-4444

This nonprofit organization operates 2 large, year-round conference centers and family resorts, both of which have been selected by *Family Circle* magazine as one of the Family Resorts of the Year.

Snow Mountain Ranch near Winter Park, Colorado, and Estes Park Center in the Colorado Rockies both have full-time program departments that give visitors an opportunity to study nature in nature. Participation can be through either a group experience such as a large family reunion or club retreat or a family vacation. Either way members get a chance to enjoy outdoor education opportunities that will leave them with a lifetime of memories.

The natural world is exposed through discovery and hands-on experiences led by professional educators. Whether in a Hug-a-Tree class or a Star Challenger course, participants will discover and enjoy an interdisciplinary, environmentally conscious approach to learning.

Tour Agencies and Lodges

In the past 20 years there has been an explosion of specialized travel companies and lodges that cater to travelers who wish to learn more about the natural history of a region in an informal way while taking a somewhat traditional tour.

Below are organizations that offer such travel opportunities. A large number of these provide customized trips according to the needs of the participants, rather than fitting participants into prearranged tours.

Credit can often be arranged for these tours through local colleges and universities.

Tour Agencies

Abercrombie & Kent

1520 Kensington Road
Oak Brook, IL 60521-2106

708-954-2944
800-323-7308

Although this company is famous for its luxurious African safaris, it has branched out to offer tours throughout the world. Many of these focus on the natural history of the region they cover. Write or call for their most recent brochures.

Alaska Discovery

369 South Franklin Street
Juneau, AK 99801

907-586-1911
FAX 907-586-2332

Alaska Discovery leads groups of 8 to 12 people on adventure vacations that involve sea kayaking, rafting and hiking, and photo expeditions to see Alaska's wildlife close up. They also offer a 10-day trip that emphasizes the natural history of Glacier Bay.

Trips are from 4 to 12 days and cost between $800 and $2,400.

Alaska Rainforest Tours

369 South Franklin Street, Suite 200
Juneau, AK 99801

907-463-3466 or 463-4453
FAX 907-463-4961

This small company offers day hikes, kayak outings, and combined tours for small groups (1 to 6 people) that explore the Alaskan rain forest around Juneau and West Chichagof Island. These can be combined to include a complete vacation, and the company is willing to develop a special tour for small groups.

104

Three travelers explore the Alaskan Rainforest. (*Photo courtesy of Alaska Rainforest Tours*)

Amazonia Expeditions, Inc.

1824 NW 102nd Way
Gainesville, FL 32606

904-332-4051

The owners of Amazonia Expeditions, Paul Beaver, Ph.D., and Milly Sangama, are fully qualified jungle guides, and one or the other accompanies every trip.

Each trip (limited to 15 people) is tailored to the needs of individual participants and can focus on special interests such as plant or insect collecting, nature photography, scientific research, fishing, birding, or anthropology.

Trips are 15 days long and cost about $1,800, which includes round-trip airfare from Miami to the Amazon.

American Museum of Natural History—Discovery Tours

Central Park West at 79th Street
New York, NY 10024-5192

212-769-5700
800-462-8687
FAX 212-769-5755

The American Museum of Natural History, as do many other museums and zoos around the country, offers organized tours to many parts of the world. These tours are generally led by natural history experts.

Contact Discovery Tours to get information on length and cost of tours.

American Wilderness Experience, Inc.

PO Box 1486
Boulder, CO 80306

303-494-2992
FAX 303-494-2996

Trips offered here are primarily wilderness adventures in the American West, Mexico, Hawaii, and South America with a little natural history thrown in. They also offer several trips to Hawaii and Peru that focus on the study of the ecology and natural history of the regions.

Trips are 7 to 22 days long and cost from $1,000 to $2,500.

Back to Nature
1420 North Stanley Avenue, Suite 205
Los Angeles, CA 90046

213-883-7808
FAX 213-851-7937

Back to Nature is an organization designed to provide small groups of travelers with a once-in-a-lifetime opportunity to experience the Amazon rain forest firsthand.

Headed by the legendary expedition leader Yossi Gihinsberg, each group voyages to the lowlands of Bolivia and camps in the lagoon territory of the Chiman Indians. From this base, participants are encouraged to choose their own explorations. Potential activities include land cruiser trips, jungle tracking, river canoeing, camera safaris, gold panning, wildlife encounters, and balsa rafting.

The group also maintains a cultural emphasis, as local tribesmen and women provide instruction in the way of life of the rain forest, and in native handicrafts.

Road and river transportation, first-class accommodation in La Paz, gourmet local delicacies, and a full-time staff of doctors, guides, cooks, and helpers are all included in the tour's cost. Prices begin at $3,600. Extensions and optional tours in South America are also available. Each expedition is limited to 14 people.

Biological Journeys
Whale Watching and Natural History Expeditions
1696 Ocean Drive
McKinleyville, CA 95521

707-839-0178
FAX 707-839-4656

This small travel organization was formed in the early 1980s and focuses on marine natural history. It leads trips to the Galapagos, Ecuador (where it conducts tours at a jungle camp), Baja California, Australia, British Columbia, and Alaska.

Most groups are small, led by trained naturalists, and travel aboard chartered boats with private and semi-private cabins. Food is generally excellent.

Recent trips have been for 8 to 22 days and have ranged in price from just over $1,000 to almost $5,000, plus airfare to staging area.

Bolder Adventures, Inc.

PO Box 1279
Boulder, CO 80306

303-443-6789
800-397-5917

Bolder Adventures only offers trips to Thailand and Indonesia, and these are guided small-group programs that are customized to meet the needs of the participants.

Most trips are from 15 to 22 days and cost between $1,500 and $4,000.

Brazilian Views, Inc.

201 East 66th Street, 21G
New York, NY 10021

212-472-9539

Brazilian Views is the sole representative for the Project Mountain Cloud Forest Field Studies programs. See Project Mountain Cloud Forest Field Studies in Canada and Abroad section for more information.

CAL Adventures

2301 Bancroft Avenue
Berkeley, CA 94720

415-642-4000

This program is the outdoor education and water safety education component of the Department of Recreational Sports at the University of California, Berkeley, campus. Everyone is eligible to participate in the trips and classes offered, however, without any requirements of UC affiliation.

The director of the program ascribes to the proverb, "Better to participate once than spectate one hundred times."

Classes and trips cover a wide range of outdoor activities, from learning basic skills in sailing and backpacking to taking natural history and photography courses.

Courses and trips last from 1 to 2 weeks and cost between $50 and $3,000.

Caligo Ventures, Inc.✦
PO Box 21
Armonk, NY 10504-0021

914-273-6333
800-426-7781

Caligo is a full-service travel agency that offers natural history tours in Belize, Venezuela, Trinidad and Tobago, Costa Rica, Panama, and Kenya. These 8- to 16-day trips cost between $1,000 and $2,300.

See Asa Wright Nature Centre in Canada and Abroad, Latin America, section.

Clearwater Trout Tours
274 Star Route
Muir Beach, CA 94965

415-381-1173

This is one of a number of tour organizations across the nation that specialize in fishing tours, but this is one with a difference. That difference is a flyfishing school that is intensive and fun. Part of the instruction at any flyfishing school, and there are many in different parts of the country, is a study of stream ecology and aquatic entomology. The programs offered by Clearwater are no exception, and participants leave the classes with a thorough knowledge of streams and their ecology.

Classes, which are held on Hat Creek in northern California, last from 2 to 5 days and cost between $350 and $900.

Participants can stay at the Clearwater House, a turn-of-the-century farmhouse near Hat Creek, for $110 to $125 per night. The latter includes 3 meals a day.

Dave Garrett Ocean Adventures
85 Liberty Ship Way
Sausalito, CA 94965
415-331-3364

Dave has been leading adventure trips (he now calls them learning adventures) worldwide since the mid-seventies, and he focuses on the areas where the land touches the sea. This includes coastal regions, islands, and even some river areas. On these trips he presents the natural history of the region while emphasizing the ecological aspects.

All the trips utilize boats for transportation, and many require some degree of sailing experience.

Trips last from 7 to 14 days and cost $800 to $2,000.

Dolphinswim
986 Acequia Madre
Santa Fe, NM 87501
505-986-0579

This program takes small groups of people to swim with a pod of wild spotted dolphins off the west coast of the Grand Bahama Islands. The group studies the natural history of the region while swimming daily with the dolphins.

A second program, Project SOS (Save Our Seas), is a nonprofit organization that takes students from all over the world and spends 6 days teaching them about environmental concerns. This program may become part of San Diego State University's experiential graduate program as a 2-unit course.

The Dolphinswim program lasts for 6 days and costs $1,400. Most SOS programs are completely subsidized by corporations and foundations. Students are informed of program costs upon acceptance.

Environmental Traveling Companions
Fort Mason Center
Landmark Building C
San Francisco, CA 94123
415-474-7662

Environmental Traveling Companions provides wilderness experiences for disadvantaged youth and people of all ages who are visually or hearing impaired or physically, emotionally, or developmentally disabled. These trips include camping, skiing, rafting, and kayaking.

Able-bodied individuals can volunteer as guides for outings to assist participants with special needs.

Eye of the Whale
Marine/Wilderness Adventures
PO Box 1269
Kapa'au, HI 96755
808-889-0227
800-657-7730

This alternative travel organization offers tourists an exciting way to vacation in Hawaii. Small groups (10 people or less) are led by 2 naturalists in a combination of sailing, snorkeling, and hiking as they learn about the natural history of Hawaii. These 10-day trips tour 3 islands (Kauai, Molokai, and Hawaii) and give participants an opportunity for hands-on experience.

Leaders Beth Goodwin and Mark Grandoni have extensive experience as naturalist leaders. Beth is a certified SCUBA instructor and Mark a USCG-licensed sea captain.

The 10-day trips are offered year-round and cost about $1,500. Five-day whale-watching tours and 6-day general tours are also offered for about $1,000.

Field Guides, Inc.

PO Box 160723
Austin, TX 78716

512-327-4953
FAX 512-327-9231

Field Guides is a birding tour company that mixes bird-watching with natural history, and recreation with travel. Their trips are worldwide and have a maximum of 16 participants with 2 guides. Trips are from 10 to 21 days and cost from $500 to $5,000. Many of these are available for college credit.

Forum International (Worldwide), Inc.

91 Gregory Lane, #21
Pleasant Hill, CA 94523

415-671-2900
FAX 415-946-1500

This nonprofit educational corporation offers over 1,200 travel programs, many of which focus on natural history.

Forum International started the International Ecology University in 1965 and can be said to have coined the word *ecotourism*. Today they offer Forum Learning Vacations and used Classroom Without Walls for some of their programs in the 1960s.

Costs vary from $600 for 8-day trips to $3,000 for 21-day trips, plus airfare.

Grand Canyon Expeditions Company

PO Box O
Kanab, UT 84741

801-644-2691

These 8-day trips traverse the Grand Canyon from Lees Ferry, Arizona (in Grand Canyon National Park), to Pearce Ferry in Lake Mead, Arizona.

Most people sign up for the standard expeditions, but the company offers a number of special-interest trips each year. These excursions follow the same course as the standard ones, but experts in ecology, geology, history, photography, archaeology, or astronomy accompany the group and share their expertise.

Special-interest expeditions run between May and September and cost about $1,500 for adults, with children between 8 and 14 years costing about $100 less. This price includes all camping equipment, transportation from Las Vegas to Lees Ferry, transportation back to Las Vegas from Lake Mead, and a deluxe menu.

Her Wild Song

PO Box 6793
Portland, ME 04101

207-773-4969

This organization offers wilderness journeys for women in Maine. Week-long studies of herbs, canoeing, meditation, and earth-centered rituals cost between $450 and $700.

Himalayan Travel, Inc.

PO Box 481
Greenwich, CT 06836

203-622-6777
800-225-2380

This full-service agency offers adventure vacation trips around the world. Their overwhelming range of tour options includes destinations such as the Himalayas, Nepal, Tibet, Egypt, Central Africa, and Malaysia. Many of them focus primarily on natural history. Costs average $60 to $100 a day, plus transportation.

InterAsia Expeditions

2627 Lombard Street
San Francisco, CA 94123
415-922-0448
800-777-8183
FAX 415-346-5535

This firm leads small tours to China (Tibet), Turkey, Bhutan, Patagonia, Nepal, and the Commonwealth of Independent States. Groups are generally no larger than 15 and sometimes as small as 5 people. Some trips are cultural in orientation, but many are led by trained naturalists and focus on the natural history of the region. These tours are given difficulty ratings as follows:

Easy: Participants stay in first-class accommodations, and there is no walking or hiking necessary.

Moderate: Accommodations have fewer conveniences; some hiking or walking is required.

Rigorous: Long drives over dirt roads, accommodations without bathrooms or hot water, and hikes above 10,000 feet are not uncommon.

They also have treks where all participants carry day packs and sleep in tents. Many trekkers have never even slept in a tent and enjoy themselves, and anyone who has spent 3 or 4 days backpacking will have no trouble on most treks. Meals are prepared by the staff.

Tours generally last from 8 to 33 days and cost from $1,600 to $7,000. Trips to the South Pole cost up to $30,000.

InterAsia also provides personalized tours for special groups and individuals.

International Zoological Expeditions, Inc.
210 Washington Street
Sherborn, MA 01770
617-655-1461

International Zoological Expeditions offers several choices of birding tours that cover Belize from the lush vegetation of the Maya Mountains through humid tropical forests and pine-covered grasslands to lowland marshes. Almost half of Belize's 500 species of birds are typically seen on a single tour. Tours are graded according to ruggedness.

Level 1: Participants stay in the best lodges in Belize and utilize the best means of air and ground transportation.

Level 2: Tours are essentially the same as Level 1 except that they include 2 nights at a rustic biological station where participants use their own sleeping bags.

Level 3: Some aspects are extremely rustic, and participants stay at a station where everyone camps out under 1 roof for 2 nights, and the site's only access is over a half-mile trail.

Tours are for 8 to 10 days and cost from $900 to $1,100.

Island Packers
1867 Spinnaker Drive
Ventura, CA 93001
805-642-7688

The Channel Islands National Park off the coast of southern California offers outstanding diving and swimming in water that nears 70 degrees during the summer and fall. The underwater sanctuary off the islands' shore has abundant marine life, and snorkeling equipment can be rented by advance arrangement on the trips offered by Island Packers.

The company offers floating field trips, seminars on island ecology, whale-watching expeditions, and 1- to 3-day island journeys year-round. These cost between $25 and $225.

Joseph Van Os Nature Tours
PO Box 655
Vashon Island, WA 98070
206-463-5362
FAX 206-463-5484

Van Os began in the early 1980s by offering tours to see polar bears at Hudson Bay and big-game herds in Kenya and Namibia. Today Van Os continues these trips but also offers tours of tropical wildlife in Belize, explorations of the wintering areas of Monarch butterflies in Mexico, wilderness trips to Alaska, and killer whale watches off remote British Columbia. They also offer over 50 photo safaris for outdoor photographers.

Tours last from 6 to 15 days and cost from $1,500 to $4,000.

Lost World Adventures
1189 Autumn Ridge Drive
Marietta, GA 30066
404-971-8586
800-999-0558
FAX 404-977-3095

Venezuela is the specialty of this company, which directs a variety of tours in the country. Many of these focus on the natural history of the region, particularly on birding.

Trips range from 3 to 12 days and cost from $300 to $2,500.

Mountain Travel

6420 Fairmont Avenue
El Cerrito, CA 94530

415-527-8100
800-227-2384
FAX 415-525-7710

Mountain Travel has offered professionally led treks, outings, and expeditions since 1969. Trips are led in Africa, Asia, the Pacific, South America, Antarctica, Europe, and Alaska.

Mountain Travel encourages whole families to participate in their tours and often makes arrangements so that younger children can participate.

Trips generally last from 8 to 33 days and cost from $900 to $6,100.

The Mountain Workshop, Inc.

PO Box 625
Ridgefield, CT 06877

203-438-3640

Sue and Corky Clark develop day-, weekend-, and week-long adventure outings for schools, businesses, and families. These involve climbing, kayaking, canoeing, wildflower studies, sailing, and caving. Costs vary from minimal to more than $1,000, depending on the program.

Natural Habitat Wildlife Adventures

1 Sussex Station, Suite 110
Sussex, NJ 07461

201-702-1525
800-543-8917

The staff consists of professional naturalists and photographers that lead participants on trips to see the world's most magnificent animals in their natural habitats.

Photographers take a playful swim with wild dolphins.
(*Photo by Steve Morello, courtesy of Natural Habitat Wildlife Adventures*)

Seal pups are easily approached, and even cuddled, by
Natural Habitat adventurers. (*Photo by Steve Morello, courtesy of
Natural Habitat Wildlife Adventures*)

Trips include the following:

Seal Watch: a visit to newborn harp seal pups in the Gulf of St. Lawrence

A polar bear observes a snow buggy full of naturalists.
(*Photo by Steve Morello, courtesy of Natural Habitat Wildlife Adventures*)

Polar Bear Watch: a visit to the tundra outside Churchill, Manitoba, on the Hudson Bay, where polar bears come within a few feet of all-terrain vehicles

Galapagos Islands: an unmatched diversity of wildlife

Primate Watch: a visit to Zaire and Rwanda to see mountain and lowland gorillas, as well as chimpanzees

Alaska and Brown Bears: a visit to a number of brown bear habitats across the state

Baja Whale Watch: a visit to the grey whales in the Sea of Cortez.

Trips last from 5 to 22 days and cost from $1,500 to $6,800.

Nature Expeditions International
474 Willamette
PO Box 11496
Eugene, OR 97440
503-484-6529
800-869-0639

Nature Expeditions International was founded in 1973. Its trips emphasize adventure, learning, and discovery in educational travel programs that range from easy explorations to physically taxing expeditions. More than 10,000 people, usually in groups of about 1 dozen, but none with fewer than 10 or more than 16, have joined NEI trips.

NEI also arranges private expeditions for museums, alumni, and zoological associations.

All NEI leaders have an M.A., Ph.D., or equivalent and college-level teaching experience. They conduct daily interpretive sessions as the group is in the field and give evening lectures and informal talks on the region being studied.

NEI leads trips worldwide and grades them according to their physical difficulty.

Easy: Stay in first-class hotels, and have leisurely walks to explore the culture and nature of a region.

Comfortable: Stay in first-class hotels, ship cabins, or deluxe tent camps and take boat trips or short day hikes of 1 to 4 miles.

Moderate: Stay in first-class hotels, comfortable tent camps, rustic lodges, small ship cabins, or village accommodations, and take boat trips or day hikes of 2 to 8 miles at altitudes below 10,000 feet.

Challenging: Stay in some first-class hotels, but mostly tent camps, mountain huts, lodges, and village accommodations, and take boat and raft trips and daily hikes of 6 to 12 miles over rugged terrain, some at altitudes between 10,000 and 16,000 feet.

Recent trips have been from 9 to 30 days and have cost between $1,500 and $5,000, plus airfare to trip staging area.

new routes, inc.
RR 5, Box 2030
Brunswick, ME 04011
207-729-7900

Since 1985 new routes has been conducting outdoor programs for women, evolving from purely recreational trips to ones that combine the teaching of outdoor skills with the development of personal, spiritual, and ecological awareness.

Trips are for 7 to 10 days and cost from $300 to $800.

Ocean Voyages Inc.
1709 Bridgeway
Sausalito, CA 94965
415-332-4681
FAX 415-332-7460

Ocean Voyages offers sailing education programs in many of the world's most ideal locations: the Aegean Sea, Corsica, Sardinia, the Grenadines, San Diego, Hawaii, the Pacific Northwest, French Polynesia, Australia, the Galapogos, New Zealand, and Costa Rica. Most of these trips also include trained naturalists who can provide information about the region as the group sails through it.

They also offer a number of tours on motor yachts in many of these locations and in Alaska.

Most of the captains are selected for their expertise as naturalists as well as for their abilities as sail trainers.

Most trips are between 3 and 15 days and cost from $500 to $3,000. There are several longer trips (Sydney to Montevideo, Montevideo to Lisbon, and Papeete to Pitcairn Island) that range in cost between $3,500 and $10,500.

Ocean Voyages is currently developing a program that will in effect be a semester-at-sea for a variety of universities. Contact them for further information.

For a description of one Ocean Voyageur's explorations, see "Transit to a Lost World" in the Vignettes section.

Outback Expeditions

PO Box 16343
Seattle, WA 98116

206-932-7012

This organization specializes in wilderness and wildlife sea-kayak tours to mainland Mexico, Baja California, Canada, and southeast Alaska. All the tours are designed for novice/intermediate kayakers and teach participants low-impact camping techniques and about the frailty of the whole ecosystems they are visiting.

Tours are from 5 to 10 days and cost from $600 to $1,100.

Outer Edge Expeditions

45500 Pontiac Trail
Walled Lake, MI 48390

313-624-5140

Outer Edge Expeditions offers small group expeditions (2 to 10 people) that include hiking, biking, backpacking, kayaking, scuba diving, and rafting. They take participants to North and South America, the Caribbean, and New Zealand.

These trips last from 8 to 15 days and cost from $1,200 to $4,400.

Pacific Exploration Company

PO Box 3042
Santa Barbara, CA 93130

805-687-7282
FAX 805-569-0722

Pacific Exploration Company offers tours to Australia and New Zealand that specialize in nature, hiking, and the outdoors, all with a nature and environmental study component. All tours are individually designed according to the clients' desires, and no 2 trips are alike.

Upon request, you are sent a booklet that describes the types of activities offered, and then you return a completed questionnaire that assists the company in personalizing a tour that includes you.

As a sample itinerary they offer an Australian walkabout that lasts for 23 days and costs $2,150 plus airfare both to and in Australia.

Pacific Quest Outdoor Adventures
PO Box 205
Haleiwa, HI 96712
808-638-8338
800-776-2518
FAX 808-638-8255

These small group programs to Hawaii and New Zealand are led by trained professionals. They are limited to 16 participants and are from 7 to 14 days long.

Pacific Sea Fari Tours
2803 Emerson Street
San Diego, CA 92106
619-226-8224
FAX 619-222-0784

Sea Fari leads tours to remote islands off Baja California and along beautiful seacoast locations. These tours take place aboard luxury sea vessels, and the natural history program is directed by Dr. Ted Walker, one of the world's foremost authorities on the California gray whale. Naturalists lead nature walks and present slide and film shows in the evenings.

Trips are for 7 to 12 days, with some 2-day trips, and cost from $250 to $2,400.

REI Adventures

PO Box 88126
Seattle, WA 98138-2126

206-395-7760
800-622-2236

REI Adventures is the travel arm of Recreational Equipment, Inc., a national retailer of outdoor gear. The company offers a number of domestic and international tours but is noted for its tours to the various countries that once comprised the Soviet Union.

Trips last from 3 to 30 days and cost between $300 and $7,000.

Sea Quest Expeditions/Zoetic Research

PO Box 2424
Friday Harbor, WA 98250

206-378-5767

Participants in this program travel by a fleet of sea kayaks around the San Juan Islands in the Pacific Northwest or in the Sea of Cortez. No special skills or previous experience are needed; if you can hike or bike, you can paddle. All expeditions are designed for whale watching.

Instructors have extensive experience in outdoor education, and most have published articles in their field of interest.

Participants must only bring their own sleeping bag, clothing, and personal items.

Trips are from 1 to 7 days long and cost from $45 to $600, plus transportation to the site.

Credits may be obtained for some trips.

Smithsonian Study Tours and Seminars
Department 0049
Washington, DC 20073-0049
202-357-4700

The Smithsonian offers 4 vastly different educational trips. The first, Smithsonian Seminars, are short 4- to 6-day programs that center around Washington, DC. The second, Smithsonian Study Tours, are 4- to 6-day tours that are held away from the Washington area. Both of these utilize experts that combine lectures with field trips. The third, Smithsonian Research Expeditions, involves participants helping scientists to conduct research activities in the field. The last, Odyssey Tours, is a traditional tour operation where participants are given a generous dose of educational lecture as they follow the tour itinerary.

These trips vary from 4 to 22 days in length and cost between $400 and $8,000.

Travelearn
PO Box 315
Lakeville, PA 18438
717-226-9114
800-235-9114

Travelearn specializes in travel/study programs for adults, and many of them concentrate on natural history. Programs are supervised by college faculty members who are specialists in the emphasized field of study. They are endorsed by over 100 universities and colleges in 31 states.

With locations around the world, Travelearn's cost is between $1,800 and $5,000, and sesssions last from 14 to 21 days.

Victor Emanuel Nature Tours
PO Box 33008
Austin, TX 78764

512-328-5221
800-328-VENT
FAX 512-328-2919

Victor Emanuel Nature Tours offers over 150 natural history tours worldwide each year. Most of these are birding tours and are led by noted experts who have had years of experience in the regions where they are instructing. Many of the tours are geared to specific birds (i.e., Arizona nightbirds, New Mexican lesser prairie chickens, etc.).

VENT also has several birding camps for young birders. One, Camp Chiricahua, is held in Arizona for 12 days in June. Another, CIELO, is held in northeastern Mexico for 12 days in July and August.

A birding workshop is held in Rockport, Texas, for 5 days in December.

Trips last from 4 to 33 days and cost from $500 to $10,000.

Voyagers International
PO Box 915
Ithaca, NY 14851

607-257-3091
FAX 607-257-3699

This tour operator leads natural history and photographic tours to Africa, Ireland, Indonesia, Antarctica, New Zealand, the Amazon, Galapagos, Central America, Hawaii, and Alaska.

Costs are between $2,000 and $6,000 for 10 to 21 days.

Wild Horizons Expeditions

West Fork Road
Darby, MT 59829

406-821-3747

Wild Horizons leads backpack trips into rugged wilderness in the Jackson Hole–Greater Yellowstone region, the central Idaho–western Montana wilderness complex, the Colorado Plateau, and the far Southwest, including parts of Arizona and New Mexico.

All guides are trained in wilderness travel, including first aid, CPR, emergency, and wilderness search and rescue procedures. They are also trained naturalists who help hikers to interpret the flora, fauna, and geology of each area.

Daily trips are usually about 7 miles long, and participants are expected to carry a 30- to 40-pound pack over rugged terrain.

Trips are generally for 1 week and cost between $600 and $800 per person. Custom and family trips can also be arranged. Contact Wild Horizons for more information about locations and costs.

Wilderness Alaska

PO Box 83044
Fairbanks, AK 99708

907-345-3567

This company primarily offers float, photography, and backpack trips in Alaska for groups that are limited to 6 participants. All trips have a natural history focus.

Costs are around $2,000 for 10-day trips. They also offer a consulting service for those planning an individual trip to Alaska and who need help with arrangements. This costs $495.

Wilderness: Alaska/Mexico

1231 Sundance Loop
Fairbanks, AK 99709

907-479-8203

Kayakers study the birds of Baja.
(*Photo courtesy of Wilderness: Alaska/Mexico*)

Ron Yarnell began leading trips to Alaska's Brooks Range in 1971 and to Mexico in 1976. He has a degree in forest recreation and is interested in birding and plant identification. Ron still leads many of the trips, and other leaders are trained naturalists.

Trips to the Brooks Range include backpacking and kayaking to some of the wildest country in North America. Those to Mexico include backpacking trips and sea kayaking.

Trips last from 8 to 22 days and cost between $1,000 and $3,000.

Wildland Adventures

3515 NE 155th
Seattle, WA 98155

206-364-0686
800-345-4453
FAX 206-363-6615

All guides for Wildland Adventures' trips are full- time residents of the country being explored. Trips are mostly to off-the-beaten-path places, and each contributes to a conservation or community development project in the host country.

Wildland is particularly experienced in Latin America, the Himalayas, and Africa.

Trips are graded as follows:

Level 1: Easy hiking and little or no camping.

Level 2: Moderate hiking, camping, and occasional steep slopes.

Level 3: Strenuous hiking, high altitude, steep slopes, and camping.

Level 4: Very strenuous hiking, with many excursions including mountaineering and technical climbing.

Trips last 3 to 21 days and range in cost from $300 to $3,100.

Womantrek

1411 East Olive Way
PO Box 20643
Seattle, WA 98102

206-325-4772
800-477-TREK

Womantrek emphasizes personal interaction with the people and natural environments of the regions explored and takes small groups of women (usually less than 15) to remote destinations where it is often difficult for women to travel alone.

Womantrek offers different types of adventures that include backpacking journeys, hiking/packing trips, bicycle trips, safaris, kayaking/rafting, skiing, and cruises. Many of these emphasize the natural history of the region.

For more travel details and a portrait of Bonnie Bordas, the owner and founder of Womantrek, see "Setting the Pace" in the Vignettes section.

Lodges

Gunflint Northwoods Outfitters
HC 64 Box 750
Grand Marais, MN 55604

800-328-3325

Gunflint has a lodge in the north woods of Minnesota, which also serves as the headquarters for wilderness canoe trips. Many of these trips specialize in wildlife and nature.

Children are welcome on many of the trips, and some trips are designed just for families.

Trips are from 4 to 7 days and cost between $200 and $700.

Lone Mountain Ranch
PO Box 69
Big Sky, MT 59716

406-995-4644

This guest ranch is located in southwest Montana about 1 hour from Yellowstone National Park. It offers a naturalist program that emphasizes the Yellowstone ecosystem, photography workshops, rock-climbing instruction, and Orvis- approved flyfishing instruction.

The ranch operates year-round and costs about $1,000 per person for 7 nights.

A couple learns the proper techniques for photographing wildflowers. (*Photo courtesy of Lone Mountain Ranch*)

Maho Bay Camps, Inc.
17 East 73rd Street
New York, NY 10021

212-472-9453
800-392-9004

This resort is a community of tent-cottages located on a private preserve within the boundaries of the U.S. Virgin Islands National Park in St. John, U.S. Virgin Islands. The cottages were built of materials carried onto the sites by hand to preserve the ground cover, and the development has won a number of awards for its ecological awareness.

Trained staff members give natural history tours and lectures, and many programs are offered by the park.

Rates are $75 per night for 2 from December 15 to April 30, and $50 from May 1 to December 14.

Mohonk Mountain House
Lake Mohonk
Lake Palz, NY 12561
914-255-1000

The Mohonk is a turreted, castle-like structure that reaches 7 stories high and stretches for almost an eighth of a mile along the shores of Lake Mohonk. It has stood for over 100 years and is designated a National Historical Landmark.

Mohonk is a full-featured resort that offers over 40 theme programs a year, many of which are naturalist in orientation. Recent programs have included The Art of Stargazing, A World of Walking, Summer Nature Week, and Birding and Spring Nature.

These programs are offered to all registered guests and last from 3 to 7 days. Room rates range from $80 to $250. When calling to inquire about rooms, mention the nature programs to find out the dates offered.

Seven Lazy P Guest Ranch
PO Box 178
Choteau, MT 59422
406-466-2044

This guest ranch houses guests in a rustic lodge made of logs and offers excellent fishing, horse-pack trips, and 3 sessions of Rocky Mountain Front Exploratory Workshops each summer. The workshops are taught by 3 trained naturalists who lead sections on birds, plants, and wildlife of the region.

Groups are limited to 12 people for the workshops, and the cost is $850 for 7 days. Contact the ranch for guest rates without workshops.

Sunriver Nature Center

PO Box 3533
Sunriver, OR 97707

503-593-4394

This nature center is part of the Sunriver resort area complex in southeastern Oregon. This complex has a full complement of resort amenities on the banks of the Deschutes River, including biking and hiking trails, tennis courts, and golf courses. The nature center is open 7 days a week between June and September and offers a wide range of nature programs for adults, older and younger children, and families. An observatory, complete with a 12-inch Osborn telescope, opened in 1991.

They have a full schedule of programs during winter vacation and offer periodic classes and workshops during fall and spring.

For more information about the resort facilities, contact the Chamber of Commerce, Sunriver, Oregon 97707.

Miscellaneous Organizations

The following workshops and classes take place outdoors but do not necessarily have instruction about natural history. These include nature photography, climbing, canoeing, and similar workshops.

Nature Photography

Anderson Ranch Arts Center
PO Box 5598
Snowmass Village, CO 81615
303-923-3181
FAX 303-923-3871

Close-Up Expeditions
1031 Ardmore Avenue
Oakland, CA 94610

415-465-8955
FAX 415-465-1237

Coupeville Arts Center
60 NW Coveland
PO Box 171
Coupeville, WA 98239

206-678-3396

Deerfield at Stonington
701 Elm Street
Essexville, MI 48732

517-893-6402

Four Seasons Nature Photography
PO Box 620132
Littleton, CO 80162

303-979-4618
303-972-1893

Frances Dorris Photography
Great Smoky Mountains Workshops
PO Box 120691
Nashville, TN 37212

615-292-6993

Global Preservation Projects
PO Box 30886
Santa Barbara, CA 93130

805-682-3398

Hulbert Outdoor Center
RR 1, Box 91A
Fairlee, VT 05045

802-333-9840

Images

PO Box 87
Gardiner, MT 59030

406-848-7749

Indian Nations International

730 Asp Avenue, Suite 211
Norman, OK 73069

800-765-6645

Indian River Photo Workshops

PO Box 7
Antwerp, NY 13608

315-659-8544

Joe McDonald Wildlife Photography

RR 2, Box 1095
McClure, PA 17841-9340

717-543-6423
215-433-7025

Macro Tours

PO Box 460041
San Francisco, CA 94146-0041

415-826-1096

Nature Photography Workshops

2210 Branch Street
Middleton, WI 53562-2841

608-831-2852

Nature's Perspective

205 Wayah Road
Franklin, NC 28734

704-369-6044
615-453-6610

Nikon Photo Programs
Waterhouse Photographic Tours
PO Box 2487
Key Largo, FL 33037

305-451-2228
800-272-9122

Northlight Photographic Workshop
362 Bullville Road
Montgomery, NY 12549

800-350-9333
914-361-1017

Osprey Photo Workshops and Tours
2719 Berwick Avenue
Baltimore, MD 21234-7616

301-426-5071

Port Townsend Photography Immersion Workshops
225 Taylor Street
Port Townsend, WA 98368

604-469-9804

Rocky Mountain School of Photography
PO Box 7605
Missoula, MT 59807-9933

406-543-0171
800-874-3686

Sierra Photographic Workshops
3251 Lassen Way
Sacramento, CA 95821

916-974-7200
800-925-2596

The 63 Ranch Photo Workshops
PO Box 979
Livingston, MT 59047

406-222-0570

Spring Nature Photography Workshop
Twin Falls Resort State Park
RR 97, Box 1023
Mullens, WV 25882

304-294-4000

Sunracer Photography
PO Box 40092
Tucson, AZ 85717

602-881-0243

Western Photo Workshops of Telluride
PO Box 968
Telluride, CO 81435

303-728-3727
FAX 303-728-6836

Wilderness Photography Expeditions
402 South 5th
Livingston, MT 59047

406-222-2302
800-521-7230

Wild Florida Photographic Workshops
502 NW 75th, Suite 384
Gainesville, FL 32607

904-375-8907

Wildlife Images Photo Tours, Inc.
8934 West Dartmouth Place
Lakewood, CO 80227

303-988-4583

Rock and Mountain Climbing Schools

Alpine Adventures, Inc.
RR 73, Box 179
Keene, NY 12942

518-576-9881

Colorado Mountain School
PO Box 2062
Estes Park, CO 80517

800-444-0730

Eastern Mountain Sports Climbing School
Main Street
North Conway, NH 03860
603-356-5433
or
2550 Arapahoe Avenue
Boulder, CO 80302

303-4427566

Mountain and Ski Adventures
PO Box 2974
Bellingham, WA 98227

206-647-0656

Outdoor Discoveries
PO Box 7687
Tacoma, WA 98407

206-759-6555

Sierra Wilderness Seminars
PO Box 707
Arcata, CA 95521

707-822-8066

Yosemite Mountaineering School
Yosemite National Park, CA 95389

209-372-1244 (September through May)
209-372-1335 (June through August)

Miscellaneous Schools

American Fishing Institute
Indiana State University
Terre Haute, IN 47809

800-234-1639

Anglers Enterprises
PO Box 2431
Edmund, OK 73083

405-348-4580

ARTA Whitewater Schools
Star Route 73
Groveland, CA 95321

209-962-7873
800-323-ARTA

California Sailing Academy, Inc.
14025 Panay Way
Marina del Rey, CA 90292

213-821-3433

L.L. Bean Flyfishing School
Freeport, ME 04033

800-341-4341, ext. 3100

Offshore Sailing School
16731 McGregor Boulevard
Fort Meyers, FL 33908

813-454-1700
FAX 813-454-1191

Orvis Flyfishing School
Historic Route 7A
Manchester, VT 05254

800-548-9548

Western Hang Gliders
PO Box 828
Marina, CA 93933

408-384-2622

Programs Based in Canada and Abroad

Canada

Arctic Edge Expeditions in the Far Northwest

Box 4850
Whitehorse, YT Y1A 4N6 Canada
403-633-5470
800-667-0366 (U.S. residents)
FAX 403-633-3820

This tour company offers canoeing, rafting, and trekking trips in the Yukon, Alaska, and the Northwest Territory. Although these are not "educational" trips as such, they do offer participants an opportunity to learn about a seldom-visited ecosystem. Guides are knowledgeable and well trained. Trips run between 6 and 15 days and cost between $750 and $2,500.

Black Feather
40 Wellington Street East
Toronto, ON M5E 1C7 Canada
416-861-1555
FAX 416-862-2314

Black Feather offers adventure trips to wilderness areas of Canada and Greenland. Participants canoe, sea-kayak, hike, and bike as they explore some of the best of the North. Trips have a maximum of 10 participants with 2 guides, both of whom are experienced in the regions toured.

Trips run between 4 and 14 days and cost between $500 and $3,000.

Bluewater Adventures
202-1656 Duranleau Street
Vancouver, BC V6H 3S4 Canada
604-684-4575
FAX 604-689-5926

This company offers natural history sailing trips during the summer along the coast from the San Juan Islands to southeast Alaska. The trips are aboard the 68-foot sailing ketch *Island Roamer,* with a crew trained in marine biology, anthropology, ornithology, and ecology. Other specialists often accompany the tours.

There are special 3-day natural history cruises offered in April and September and regular 6- to 11-day cruises between May and October. These cost between $400 and $2,600.

Butterfield & Robinson

70 Bond Street
Toronto, ON M5B 1X3 Canada

416-864-1354
800-387-1147 (from U.S.)
800-268-8415 (from Canada)
FAX 416-864-0541

This company offers physically active tours throughout the world, many of which emphasize the natural history of the region. They also offer many educational tours designed for students that are open to all. Cost and length of tours vary widely.

Canadian Nature Tours

Federation of Ontario Naturalists
355 Lesmil Road
Don Mills, ON M3B 2W8 Canada

416-444-8419
FAX 416-444-9866

Bird-banding trips to the Bahamas in the winter, observation tours of lakes, loons, and lochs in Ontario in the spring, canoeing adventures with kids on a wilderness lake in Algonquin Park in the summer, and backpacking journeys to the Algonquin Highlands in the fall are a few of the activities offered by the Federation of Ontario Naturalists.

The federation offers these tours to help members meet and to learn about and become committed to preserving the environment.

All participants must become members of the federation (about $30 per year) before joining a tour group. Trips last from 4 to 14 days and cost between $500 and $5,000.

Ecosummer Expeditions
1516 Duranleau Street
Vancouver, BC V6H 3S4 Canada
604-669-7741
FAX 604-669-3244

ECO is an acronym for "Education and Challenge in the Outdoors," and this company has been running tours developed around that philosophy since 1976.

The founder of Ecosummer realized that wilderness travel is one of the surest ways of recruiting troops to the war against environmental destruction. To stand in a cathedral of giant cedar and spruce, climb over rich intertidal zones, or snorkel among coral cities in Belize is to gain contact with the natural world and its ebb and flow.

Today the company offers a variety of trips that are graded from easy to strenuous, exploring not only the Canadian wilderness but wild places in Central and South America, Asia, and Africa as well. Many of these tours include instruction in outdoor skills and natural history.

Trips last between 6 and 25 days and cost between $1,000 and $8,500.

Educo Adventure School
PO Box 1978
100 Mile House, BC V0K 2E0 Canada
604-395-3388

or
4817 North Country Road 29
Loveland, CO 80538-9515

303-679-4309

This wilderness school features specific adventure- challenge activities that allow participants to see themselves from a new perspective. The program emphasizes inner strength, meaning, and self-reliance as participants explore a variety of outdoor activities.

Adventure school participants traverse a Canadian mountain peak.
(*Photo courtesy of Educo Adventure School*)

Although the program was developed for school-age youth, there are now offerings for young adults over the age of 18.

Educo has recently expanded their program to Colorado. For information about costs and dates of program offerings, contact either the Canadian or Colorado office.

Great Canadian Ecoventures

PO Box 9
New Denver, BC V0G 1S0 Canada

604-358-7727
800-663-8641 (from U.S.)
FAX 604-358-7262

This company operated as the East Wind Arctic Expeditions for 16 years and led groups into remote Arctic regions. In 1991 it expanded its offerings and now takes tours on the Canadian Heritage River system and to other critical wildlife-conservation areas across Canada.

Study tours, most of which include considerable canoeing, closely examine the last great wilderness areas of North America such as the Bloodvien River in Ontario and Manitoba, the Woodland Caribou Provincial Park, and the Seal River in northern Manitoba. In addition, the company will continue to lead tours in the Thelon and Kazan River valleys of the Northwest Territories.

These tours last between 9 and 20 days and cost from $3,000 to $5,000 from Minneapolis.

Huntsman Marine Science Centre
Brandy Cove
St. Andrews, NB E0G 2X0 Canada
506-529-8895
FAX 506-529-4337

Three women conduct marine research in the Bay of Fundy in Canada.
(*Photo courtesy of the Huntsman Marine Science Center*)

This center was established in 1969 and has gained a reputation for excellence in marine research and education. Located in St. Andrews, New Brunswick, at the mouth of the Bay of Fundy—one of the most biologically active bodies of water in the world—the center offers a number of educational opportunities.

The public is welcome to join a variety of educational programs that range from 1-day to 1-week field trips to longer internship

148

experiences. These are all taught through learn-by-experience methods.

Academic programs are also available through the center and its 13 member universities. Year-round courses are offered in marine sciences, plus summer field courses that may be taken for credit. A university-level, credit course in marine aquaculture is also offered.

Contact the center for costs and current offerings.

Madawaska Kanu Centre
Box 635
Barry's Bay, ON K0J 1B0 Canada
613-756-3620
FAX 613-756-3667

This was the first white-water school for kayaks and canoes in Canada, and it offers weekend and 5-day courses that range in cost between $150 and $800, depending on the options chosen.

Northern Lights Alpine Recreation
Box 399
Invermere, BC, V0A 1K0 Canada
No phone available

This small, one-man operation offers trips for small groups that involve climbing, hiking, ski touring, snowshoeing, photography, exploration, and rescue training in the wild mountain landscapes of southeastern British Columbia.

All participants bring their own food and camping/climbing/photography gear and carry their own loads into wild, rugged country.

Instruction in mountain photography and the other activities listed above is offered in the summer and winter.

Courses are for 8 to 10 days and cost about $400.

Northern Sun Tours, Ltd.

PO Box 3939
Smithers, BC V0J 2N0 Canada

604-847-4349

This company offers instruction in canoeing as well as 1- to 5-day guided canoe trips in northwestern British Columbia. They also offer some extended adventure trips that last 10 to 12 days. All of these take participants into wilderness areas where flora and fauna can be studied close up.

Parks Are for People Program

Nova Scotia Department of Lands and Forests
PO Box 698
Halifax, NS B3J 2T9 Canada

No phone available

This is a series of primarily 1-day outings and seminars on the natural history of Nova Scotia offered through the cooperative effort of various government agencies, clubs, organizations, and interested individuals, and coordinated by the Department of Lands and Forests.

These programs are offered between May and September, and many require preregistration. Contact the office listed above for information about current offerings.

Purcell Lodge

PO Box 1829
Golden, BC V0A 1H0 Canada

604-344-2639

This remote lodge sits among one of the most rugged mountain wilderness areas in Canada. Lodgers' outdoor experience begins even before they arrive, as they must either make a 4- to 5-hour hike or take a 15-minute helicopter flight to reach their destination. Located at 7,200 feet on the boundary of Canada's Glacier National

Students pause to appreciate the natural history of a remote alpine ecosystem at Purcell Lodge near Golden, British Columbia.
(*Photo courtesy of ABC Wilderness Adventures Ltd.*)

Park, the lodge offers easy access to high peaks and montane meadows covered with wildflowers.

Although most of the natural history instruction covered by the staff and guides is unstructured and informal, guests do learn much about topics relevant to the environment. There is also instruction in a variety of self-propelled outdoor pursuits such as backpacking, skiing, snowshoeing, and climbing.

Cost per night, per person ranges between $110 and $170. This includes everything except souvenirs, alcoholic beverages, and soft drinks.

Clubs and other agencies often use the lodge for formal courses and seminars, and they are planning to develop more formal educational activities since the demand is increasing. Contact them for current information.

Sail North

PO Box 2497
Yellowknife, NWT X1A 2P8 Canada
403-873-8019
FAX 403-873-6387

The sailing courses offered by Sail North are provided by the Canadian Yachting Association, and the company is Canada's northernmost charter embarkment. Courses and charters take place on Great Slave Lake, the third largest lake in North America. The charters and sailing courses also emphasize natural and human history of the Great Slave Lake region.

Courses are offered at beginning, intermediate, and advanced levels. A 2-week-long beginner's course costs $399. Charters range from hour-long rentals for $37.50 to 7-night guided excursions for $1,099.

Contact the company for more specifics about current offerings and costs.

Strathcona Park Lodge and Outdoor Education Centre

PO Box 2160
Campbell River, BC V9W 5C9 Canada
604-286-8206
FAX 604-286-6010

This lodge was built with the goal of incorporating environmental education into all aspects of its operations. Today thousands of students, from elementary school classes through Elderhostel programs for senior citizens, come to the lodge, which sits on 160 acres of private land adjacent to the vast wilderness of Strathcona Provincial Park in the middle of Vancouver Island, to participate in outdoor educational activities.

These engagements range from weekend trips for the whole family to 5-month-long leadership-training programs at the Canadian Outdoor Leadership Training Centre.

Costs vary with the programs. Some cost as little as $200, and others, such as the 5-month-long leadership program, cost up to $6,500.

Contact the lodge for a listing of current activities.

Whistler Centre for Business and the Arts
Box 1172
Whistler, BC V0N 1B0 Canada
604-932-8310
FAX 604-932-4461

This center was established in 1988 as a nonprofit educational society and provides a variety of programs at a beautiful mountain resort about 90 miles north of Vancouver. Among the programs offered at the center are nature photography workshops that feature such instructors as Galen Rowell, Robert Frutos, Pat Morrow, Robert Stahl, and Bruce Barnbaum.

These 2- to 5-day workshops cost between $300 and $600. Accommodations and food are not included in this price.

Wildlife Tours, Ltd.
227 Wright Street
Fredericton, NB E3B 2E3 Canada
506-459-7325
FAX 506-453-3589

This company offers guided tours to exciting wildlife areas of the North. Destinations include North Baffin Island in the spring and summer, Prince Edward Island to view harp seal pups, and North Labrador for a Caribou Tundra adventure.

These tours are from 7 to 10 days and cost between $1,500 and $5,000.

Great Britain

Borrobol Lodge
Kinbrace
Sutherland, Scotland KW11 6UB U.K.
No phone available

Birding at Borrobol introduces guests to the avifauna of the northern Highlands of Scotland. The lodge sits on an 8,700-hectare estate in the heartland of the roaming red deer, and in the spring over 100 species of birds can be seen there. These include most of the raptors found in Great Britain, as well as many seabirds. The private, secluded estate grounds are mainly open heather moorland with areas of woodland, grassland, a river valley, and 2 lochs.

An experienced ornithologist guides all groups of birders on field trips that explore Borrobol and the surrounding areas.

The lodge is one of the most attractive private baronial houses in Sutherland, the least populated county in the British Isles. It is a wood-paneled Edwardian sporting lodge with a library of bird books, stuffed birds, and numerous paintings by the foremost British bird artists of the last 150 years.

There are 6 bedrooms and 3 bathrooms for guests, plus 2 drawing rooms and a large dining hall. A professional chef caters to guests with a menu of local fish and game. Wine and spirits are provided in the cost.

Birding season generally includes May, June, and the first part of July.

Guests pay about $1,600 for 1 week at the lodge, and this price covers all activities, room, and meals. Day trips to Orkney are also arranged.

U.S. residents contact: Josephine Barr, 519 Park Avenue, Kenilworth, Illinois 60043; 708-251-4110 (Illinois), 800-323-5463 (outside Illinois) for current information. Canadian residents contact: Jerome Knap, Global Expeditions, 87 Mill Street, Almonte, ON K0A 1AD; 613-256-4057.

Coleg Harlech
Harlech, Gwynedd LL46 2PU Wales

011-44-0766-780363

The 1-week summer sessions offered by this campus in the Snow-donia National Park cover a variety of subjects, and one is the Ecology of Snowdonia National Park. This course consists primarily of field trips to the various habitats found in this part of Wales. Students study beach and sand-dune systems, deciduous and coniferous forests, upland lakes and streams, and heaths and moorlands.

Full cost of the 1-week sessions, including tuition, room, board, and transportation to field trips, is about $500.

Field Studies Council
Central Services
Preston Montford
Montford Bridge, Shrewsbury SY4 1HW U.K.

011-44-0743-850674

The Field Studies Council is a clearinghouse for information about course offerings in natural history and allied studies at 9 separate residential field centers around the United Kingdom. Each center is located in pleasant countryside where participants can get together with others who share their interest in learning more about some aspect of the outdoor environment. The centers have been operating for over 40 years, and each is headed by a warden and director of studies who are qualified to teach the academic subjects offered. Some courses are taught by full-time center staff, while others are taught by visiting experts.

Participants stay in accommodations furnished by the centers, some of which are very new, and activities are essentially communal, with everyone sharing preparations and cleanup.

Courses offered cover topics such as general natural history, biology and conservation, birds and other animals, flowers and other plants, geology, landscape and climate, archaeology, history and architecture, painting and drawing, and photography and crafts.

The centers are listed below, along with their locations and special areas of interest.

Dale Fort Field Centre
Haverfordwest, Dyfed SA62 3RD U.K.

011-44-0646-636205

The converted military fortification stands on the tip of a narrow peninsula jutting into Milford Haven. The magnificent cliff scenery, of considerable geological interest, is broken by sandy bays and rocky coves of widely differing degrees of exposure to the Atlantic. Opportunities for exploring shore and marine biology are unsurpassed. Inland habitats are many and varied.

Flatford Mill Field Centre
East Bergholt
Colchester, Essex CO7 6UL U.K.

011-44-0206-298283

This center lies on the Suffolk side of the River Stout near the head of tidal water, in the heart of the farmlands of Constable's country. Above the 18th-century mill, the meandering river, numerous ponds, and dikes afford excellent opportunities for aquatic biology. Below the mill are stretches of salt marsh and extensive mudflats attractive to migrating ducks and waders. Interesting sections of the North Sea coast are easily accessible.

Juniper Hall Field Centre
Dorking, Surrey RH5 6DA

011-44-0306-883849

Situated on National Trust land around Box Hill, this center offers immediate access to one of the finest wild areas of the North Downs and is also well placed for excursions into the forest and heath country of the Western Weald—a region of great geographical diversity with a wide variety of plant and animal life. Within a few miles of the center are samples of almost every type of inland habitat found in southern England.

Malham Tarn Field Centre
Settle, North Yorkshire BD24 9P
011-44-072-93-331

This center occupies an imposing site above the shores of the 153-acre tarn on a 1,300-foot plateau of carboniferous limestone. The region is of strong geological interest, and Malham Moor offers an astonishing variety of vegetation types and animal habitats. These range from peat systems to limestone grassland, and from shallow calcareous waters of the Tarn and stony-hill streams to acid peat pools.

Nettlecombe Court
The Leonard Wills Field Centre
Williton, Tauton, Somerset TA4 4HT
011-44-0984-40320

Nettlecombe Court is a beautiful part-Elizabethan mansion that lies secluded in a sheltered west Somerset valley between the Brendon Hills and the Bristol Channel. This unspoiled corner of the country rests on the boundary between upland and lowland Britain and offers excellent opportunities for geological fieldwork. A wide range of terrestrial and freshwater habitats supplemented by the unusual seashores of the Bristol Channel is enticing for biologists.

Orielton Field Centre
Pembroke, Dyfed SA71 5EZ
011-44-9646-661225

This center is set in a wooded estate of 54 acres in a corner of the Angle Peninsula 2 miles south of Pembroke. The countryside is of great variety and beauty, with the coastline included in a national park. To the north are the sheltered shores of Milford Haven, with salt marshes and extensive mudflats, and to the south lie the magnificent limestone cliffs of the Atlantic shore. Blown sand, woodland, ponds, and streams complete the variety of habitats available for study nearby.

Preston Montford Field Centre

Montford Bridge, Shrewsbury SY4 1DX

011-44-0743-850380

This center sits in a pasture and overlooks a quiet section of the River Severn in the North Shropshire lowlands. Farmland, meres, mosses, and canals in the lowland area create a countryside in striking contrast to the neighboring wild hills of South Shropshire and the Welsh border country.

Rhyd-Y-Creuau

The Drapers' Field Centre
Betws-y-coed, Gwynedd LL24 0HB Wales

011-44-069-02-494

The center is situated in the lower Conwy Valley a mile northeast of Betws-y-coed. The fault-guided valley separates the Denbigh moors, on Silurian rocks, to the east from the more rugged igneous and pre-Silurian rocks of Snowdonia to the west. The north Welsh coast, with its outcrops of carboniferous limestone, is accessible. Habitats within walking distance include acid-sessile-oak woodland plantations of various ages, moorland and rocky heath, mountain meadows, improved lowland pastures, and soft-water streams.

Slapton Ley Field Centre

Slapton, Kingsbridge, Devon TQ7 2QP U.K.

011-44-0548-580466

The site of this center is a small, typically Devonian village straddling a sheltered valley that drains into a freshwater lake, Slapton Ley. The Ley is separated from the sea by a 2½-mile bank of shingle known as the Slapton Sands. Both are within the center's 460-acre nature reserve, which also includes 2 large, deciduous woods drained by swift streams. In addition, there is easy access to rocky shores and estuarine mudflats.

All residential courses offered by the Field Studies Council generally last between 2 and 10 days and cost between $150 and $500. In addition to the residential centers, the council runs a number of courses overseas under the auspices of the Field Council Overseas program. These courses last between 1 and 4 weeks and cost between $1,500 and $8,000. Contact the council for a full listing of courses currently offered.

Knuston Hall Residential College for Adult Education

Irchester, Wellingborough
Northants NN9 7EU U.K.

011-44-0933-312104
FAX (0933) 57596

The Northamptonshire County Council has sponsored adult education courses at Knuston Hall since 1951. The hall is an elegant building set in the countryside of central Northamptonshire, and it provides a full range of teaching facilities.

Courses offered are open to anyone over 19 years of age and are directed toward participants with a lively interest in a subject rather than those with previous experience or academic preparation.

The college offers several hundred weekend and week-long courses each year. A number of these cover natural history topics such as Wildlife and Natural History Photography, Woodlands in Springtime, Birds in Springtime, and Painting From Nature.

Weekend courses generally cost about $125 and week-long ones about $300.

University of Birmingham
School of Continuing Studies
Edgbaston, Birmingham B15 2TT U.K.
011-44-021-414-5605

The programs offered through this university are very similar to what you find in American universities. Most classes are held 1 day a week for a number of weeks, but some are nonresidential weekend programs. Other courses offered by the university are short 1-day or weekend courses, residential programs, and study tours. All of these courses are open to the general public, and many focus on natural history topics.

Detailed brochures on the residential courses and study tours are available upon request. A catalog of current continuing education courses is also available.

France

These following two organizations will provide information on any programs in France where you can study about nature in nature. You can then contact the individual programs to learn about courses offered, where they are located, and what they will cost. Note that these organizations will probably answer your queries in French and expect those who participate in their programs to speak French.

Ligue Française pour la Protection des Oiseaux (LPO)

(League for the Protection of Birds)
La Corderie Royale
BP 263, 17305 Rochefort Cédex France

011-33-1-46-99-59-97

Contact this organization if you are interested in birding activities in France.

Société Nationale de la Protection de la Nature (SNPN)

(National Society for the Protection of Nature)
57 rue Cuvier, B.P. 405, 75231 Paris Cédex 05 France
011-33-1-47-07-31-95

This is France's oldest conservation organization, and it provides a number of services to interested naturalists.

Latin America

Asa Wright Nature Centre and Lodge
c/o Caligo Ventures, Inc.
387 Main Street
PO Box 21
Armonk, NY 10504-0021
914-273-6333
800-426-7781

Asa Wright Nature Centre is located at a 1,200-foot elevation in the mountains of the northern range of Trinidad and was established to provide a recreation and study area relating to tropical wildlife. The center is open to all.

Spring Hill Estate, where the center is located, is a cocoa-coffee-citrus plantation partly reclaimed by secondary forest and is surrounded by rain forest where some climax areas have an upper-story canopy 100 to 150 feet high.

Trinidad has 108 mammal, 400 bird, 55 reptile, 25 amphibian, and 617 butterfly species. Experienced birders often add 120 to 150 species to their "life-list" during a short stay.

Field trips of Trinidad are offered by the center, as well as summer seminars in tropical field natural history, bird study, and nature photography.

Costs are $500 to $1,200 plus airfare for 7- to 10-day trips. Caligo often offers special trips that are less expensive that include airfare.

Explorama Tours
Exploraciones Amazonicas S. A.
Box 446
Iquitos, Peru
011-51-23-5471
FAX 23-4968

This company operates tours and lodges in the Peruvian rain forests and conducts a number of natural history programs. Explorama Inn is located about 25 miles downstream from Iquitos on the Amazon River and is the newest, most modern lodge operated by the company; Explorama Lodge is 50 miles downstream on the Amazon deep in the jungle and offers a more primitive experience to travelers; and Explonapo Camp is located in the Sucusari Nature Reserve about 100 miles from Iquitos. This 20,000-acre reserve is privately owned by Explorama.

A number of natural history programs are offered at these lodges. For more than 20 years a UCLA extension course, taught by Dr. Mildred Mathias and other UCLA professors, has been offered for credit and noncredit at the lodges. California State University, Sacramento, also offers language and natural history courses.

Explorama Tours first conducted what it hopes to be an annual "Rainforest Workshop" in March 1991. This 8-day workshop can be taken either on a credit or noncredit basis.

In addition to these formal courses, guests at the lodges can participate in many natural history tours and programs that are led by guides employed by Explorama. These guides are all natives of the rain forests in the Amazon Basin and have learned information that complements their native knowledge from scientists who have worked in the region.

Explorama also is one of a group of private companies and individuals that have joined together to form the Foundation for the Conservation of the Peruvian Amazon Biosphere. The foundation maintains the Amazon Biosphere Reserve, which is adjacent to the Sucusari Reserve. The reserve now contains more than 250,000 acres, and by 1995 the foundation hopes to have more than 1 million acres protected. A scientific laboratory, the Amazon Center for Environmental Education and Research, is being developed by the foundation. This center will include a lab for scientists, as well as quarters for scientists and visitors.

A significant feature of the lab will be a 300-yard-long canopy walkway that will be 100 feet above the ground. This walkway will be accessible to all visitors who can get a bird's-eye view of the rain forest without the need for special climbing gear.

Costs begin at $385 for a full week of lodging. Courses cost extra.

Project Mountain Cloud Forest Field Studies

c/o Brazilian Views, Inc.
201 East 66th Street, 21G
New York, NY 10021-6451

212-472-9539

In early 1990, 17,500 acres of the Mata Atlantica Amazon rain forest in Brazil were declared a historic nature preserve. Part of this preserve is the Mountain Cloud Forest. In early 1991, the first field study project in the preserve was held with 15 students and 5 teachers from the Edinburgh Academy in Scotland and 2 professors from Edinburgh University. They spent 20 days in the preserve involved with a variety of projects, and 1 professor discovered 20 new species of moths during his stay.

Graduate, undergraduate, and high-school students, as well as scientists and amateur naturalists are all welcome to participate in the field studies programs at Mt. Cloud. They are led by Dr. Richard Warren and David Miller, who are ornithologists and biologists, and C. M. Fitch, an award-winning photographer and horticulturalist.

Programs are held from February through April and from late August through December. Participants stay in either the main house or the bunkhouse and are furnished all meals. Price is $1,200 per person based on groups of 15 people and does not include airfare to Brazil. Individuals might be placed with others to form a group of 15 to keep costs lower.

II

Vignettes

Wordscapes—Northland College's Outdoor Writing Institute Takes Shape

Northland College

"I wanted to learn who I am, and I found that my search always took me back to the natural world. Writing about nature helped me learn about myself."

—Jim Williams, a 1990 Wordscapes student.

When Jim Williams, a Yale sophomore, sat down in Bobb Hall last August for the first session of Wordscapes, he probably looked around the room and wondered if he was in the right place. Thirty people representing three generations surrounded him, and as the introductions revealed personal information, it became obvious that there wasn't a "typical" student in the group. True, each person had come to the 12-day intensive writing workshop to force him- or herself to write better, but each came with a very different agenda.

Take Jim. He had just arrived from a two-month stewardship of a 10-acre island in the middle of Chesapeake Bay, and he wanted to write a long interpretive article about that experience. Others in the group had intriguing backgrounds and interests, too:

Lee Boland, a civil engineer on the verge of retiring, signed up to try something completely different from his daily job and family routine.

Ann Sterzinger, a soft-spoken high-school sophomore and already a prodigious writer, expressed her eagerness to participate in the dawn excursions to the Fish Creek slough.

Scott Fuller, a recent high-school graduate, wanted to hone his writing skills before enrolling in the Ringling Brothers and Barnum and Bailey Clown College in Florida.

Mary Callendar, a recent UW–Stevens Point graduate, came in search of ghosts in the Apostle Islands.

Kathy Campbell, a homemaker, took the class to overcome her fears of crossing a large body of open water in a small boat.

Terri Walker came from urban Philadelphia for an annual soul trek.

Jeff Rennicke, chief writer-in-residence for Wordscapes and designer of its unique curriculum, had plans to meet all their needs. Along with coordinator Mary Rehwald, he designed a daily schedule aimed at removing participants from regular "known" worlds and placing them in a new space to explore and write from. The organizers knew that the mysterious process of getting one's pen to move creatively across a blank page is a challenge that can be approached with as many strategies as there are aspiring writers.

Undaunted by the challenge to nourish each person's muse, Rennicke and Rehwald planned for field trips—one to Waverly Beach to learn the ways of the Chippewa, one to Bayfield to practice the art of interviewing, and one to the Sigurd Olson Environmental Institute (a co-sponsor of Wordscapes) to study the writings of Sigurd Olson.

For many, a three-day trip to the Apostle Islands highlighted the experience. Students went in their choice of a voyager canoe (seating for 16), a kayak, or a sailboat. Those who felt closest to the water during their journey to the islands (the kayakers) were most likely to write about it in their final essays. Stephanie Peterson began her essay this way: "I danced with something so powerful it has wrecked large ships."

Once ashore, the students continued their introspective writing, some underscoring what well-known Wyoming writer Gretel Ehrlich believes—that nature writers can only be tutored by the land:

It isn't the landscape that matters so much as the way you live in it. You have to take some kind of step out of your own known world. You are not ever really going to know anything or anyone or any place unless you go there in some naked state emotionally and physically.

The 1991 Wordscapes institute is poised for a repeat performance of last year's deep introspection. It is scheduled from August 1 to 13—one extra day has been added to accommodate a four-day visit to the Apostles. Coordinator Mary Rehwald anticipates "that each new class will inspire exploration, adventure, humor, and serious reflection."

The first night that I met Jim Williams he told me that he went to Yale, so I immediately assumed he was a pompous ass. Somehow seeing him in the back of a Bronco . . . and raise his arm high enough so that his lips could touch the inner arm opposite his elbow and then blow so hard that the voices he made did not even sound human; somehow, I got a new perspective on Jim. He spent a lot of his time here reading, in fact, we've only been here two weeks and he has already read five books—5 real books with no pictures and lots of pages.

Adapted (with permission) from an article by Marie Marriggi first published in The Highway.

The Chance of a Lifetime

Outdoor Semester in the Rockies
Colorado Mountain College

The camp stirred slowly in the December morning as the sun stubbornly refused to peek over the high ridge. Todd Burris and other students emerged from their frost-covered tents to start camp stoves for a breakfast of "bear mush" and a cup of hot chocolate. They had been outdoors for most of three months, and winter camping along the Continental Divide was their final test.

Outdoor Semester in the Rockies

It had begun early in September in these same mountains— Colorado's Sawatch Range. Todd and 18 other students with nothing in common had come together to learn about themselves, about working with each other, and about the natural environment. They came from Stockton, California, and Bremerton, Washington; Durango, Colorado, and other states. Few had experience in the mountains. So Dr. Jim Campbell *gave* them experience—28 days in the wilderness with nothing but a backpack.

171

During that time they learned how to find their way through the mountains with a map and compass. They learned to identify the plants, trees, and wildlife. They stood on the summit of a 14,000-foot peak. And they spent three days alone on a mountainside.

"The solo was a good time to get my mind clear and put my thoughts together," says Todd. "It was so peaceful. All I had was my pen, my paper, and my thoughts. It made me look at things differently, made me a little more human."

The group welcomed the fall equinox in the Utah desert. Camped on the edge of Mule Canyon, they could see hundreds of miles in any direction across the red slickrock and sand. As the sun dipped low in the giant sky, the magic began. Balanced on the western horizon, the sun swelled into a giant orange ball, setting the desert's red sandstone on fire. On the eastern horizon, exactly opposite the sun, a golden lunar disk climbed into the evening sky.

"The desert and the whole sky turned pink," Todd remembers.

"There were cliff dwellings all around in the canyon below us," says Chris Topness of Bremerton, Washington. "We sat around the campfire and sang beneath the moon so bright you could read a book."

Later, the group spent several days hiking through Grand Gulch, another Utah canyon where dozens of cliff dwellings lie still, undisturbed.

"It seemed like dropping right out of the world," Chris recalls. "Nothing was there to tell you it was 1990."

A few weeks later they were in the middle of 1990 as they found themselves driving the wrong way down the Baja 1000 race course in Mexico.

"We just turned down a backroad, and all of a sudden race cars started coming at us across the desert on a one-way road," Linnea Sherman recalls. "The course wasn't marked at all."

The group had traveled to Mexico to study marine biology on the Gulf of California and to compare the culture of Mexican Indian villages to the archeological sites they had studied throughout the Southwest. Three weeks later they were climbing frozen waterfalls.

"Winter survival" was the name of the final section. Students who had never been on cross-country skis would learn the telemark

172

turn, then ski into the frozen wilderness a week later with enough gear and food for five days.

The December sun was fading early as Todd and his team threw the last few shovels of snow on top of their snow shelter. They sat down for a rest before digging out an entrance and sleeping platforms in the snow mound where they would spend the night.

Soon it would be dark again. And cold. The pale light of winter had barely melted the frost on their tents. But inside they held the warmth of the semester. A semester of challenges. A semester of accomplishments. A semester of turning the impossible into new possibilities.

In three days they would pack up camp and point their skis downhill toward the ghost town of Saint Elmo and the final celebration at Mt. Princeton Hot Springs. Many would leave with a new direction.

Before Outdoor Semester, Chris was unsure about continuing in college. New he has returned to Washington to earn a psychology degree and eventually counsel troubled kids through outdoor programs. Todd came here with little idea about his future. But after spending three months outdoors, he wants to work toward preserving the environment for the next generation. So he's continuing on in the Colorado Mountain College Environmental Technology program.

"If you want to experience the chance of a lifetime, something you will never forget," says Todd, "then Outdoor Semester in the Rockies is for you."

Adapted (with permission) from an article first published in Inside Edge.

The University of Wild

Wilderness Institute
University of Montana

Writing this ought to be a simple matter of summarizing a fully accredited college program dedicated to the study of wilderness, a sort of University of Backpacking, if you will. No big deal. But what do I do about these three naked people who seem to have slipped into my story?

The rub is that this nudity was in a classroom, the result of an assignment, a revealing thesis relevant to the topic at hand, and now you see my problem. The issue here is "wild," not as in "wild and crazy," the ethic that rules ordinary run-of-the-frat-house college debauchery. This is about "wild" as in "wild and free," a notion not easily reduced to words, or for that matter, to a college curriculum. Still, the University of Montana has been trying the latter feat for 16 years, and therein we find our tale.

My brush with this story began in the late summer of 1989, when I was, as the euphemism goes, between jobs. I'd been an environmental reporter for a newspaper, which had created in me more than a passing interest in the concepts of wilderness and the backcountry, especially as they related to the Northern Rockies—my neck of the woods. That made me a sucker for a flyer I spotted one day on UM's campus in my hometown of Missoula. It detailed a program called Wilderness and Civilization.

Had I considered this fully at the time, I probably would have deduced that studying wilderness and civilization is a bit like studying math and everything that is not math: a global undertaking. I didn't, though. Instead I read the "wilderness" part. I read how courses would be conducted during extended backpacking trips. I read how hiking, which I'd be doing anyway on my own for fun, could translate into two full semesters of real and negotiable college credit. There were phrases like "using as a classroom over five million acres of wilderness in the wild Rockies" and photos of robust and blond young persons bearing backpacks. The word "scam" came to mind, so I signed up for higher education as it occurs in high mountain passes. Call me curious.

Classes began in September amid a pile of backpacks, gaiters, stuffsacks and the sundry accoutrements of the hip-and-happening backcountry sojourner. On a rainy afternoon 25 of us piled our gear in a classroom, which was to be our last indoor activity for two weeks. Other than the old guy (I openly confess to being thirty-something), the students were mostly in their early twenties. Skill levels ranged from graduates of and instructors for the National Outdoor Leadership School all the way to total idiots, which explains why so much equipment was piled in the classroom.

The goal was to gather 25 post-teens-adventurers and flakes alike—and dump them in the grizzly-infested reaches of the Bob Marshall Wilderness. Alan McQuillan, director of the program and the university's Wilderness Institute, said 16 years of experience has taught organizers to expect the idiot factor to occasionally loom large. A few years back the group headed out for two weeks only to find one rotund pilgrim had packed frozen pizzas as her sole provisions for the duration. Since then organizers have carefully inspected gear and food.

Still, instructors avoid planning and supervision, largely so students can make their own mistakes. The philosophy is to let the wilderness teach; instructors stay out of the way. For instance, the faculty doesn't teach backcountry skills. The program is not simply a college-accredited version of NOLS.

The program also does not train students for jobs. Not that the study of wilderness doesn't have its practical side. Most formally designated wilderness areas are under the purview of the Forest Service. That agency is overly fond of the word "management" and hires people to attend to the care and feeding of wilderness areas. You can receive such training at the University of Montana in other programs, but McQuillan is blunt in refusing to run a trade school.

"I got some flak from the faculty in the forestry school for not including more recreation than I did, but it (the program) is not going to be about recreation," he says. "It's not going to be about where you put the picnic tables and how people trample down grass in campgrounds and that stuff. Personally, I don't have a lot of time for those kinds of courses. I call that 'picnic-table-management'."

As students, we talked not at all about management, especially during those first two weeks. That first trip was as advertised. We simply went backpacking. We split into small hiking groups, aimed for widely separated trailheads, then rode Suburbans to an area along the Eastern Front of the Rockies just south of Glacier National Park. Each group spent two weeks hiking 70 miles or so of the Bob Marshall and an adjacent undesignated wilderness called the Badger Two-Medicine, a stretch of sacred geography vital to the religious traditions of the Blackfeet people.

As well it should be, for in that area we found the sort of achingly beautiful backcountry that can cradle one's soul. Except for a rendezvous at midtrip when the groups converged to swap car keys and stories, there were no classes or academic duties. Our assignment was to roam and to breathe the wilderness we would study for the next six months. This trip was education at its finest, I decided one cloudless morning beside a lake that mirrors the peaks of the Continental Divide. My instructors that class period were a great horned owl, a beaver that wedged the lake's surface, and a pair of moose that gamboled out from the trees. More enlightening pedagogy I have not known.

After the trip I was to know more conventional teaching, but that day I lazed around camp wrapped in Huck Finn-ish calculations, wondering whether this two weeks of bliss would compensate for the considerable pile of serious book learnin' that lay ahead. It was not idle speculation, because "serious" considerably understates the case.

The fall semester's gamut included a hard-science course on environmental problems and an economics course designed to give at least an equal commercial footing to preservation of wild lands. Two other courses examined the philosophical and legal history of environmental regulation, especially as it pertains to the Forest Service. One was taught by Bob Ream, a nationally respected wolf biologist and McQuillan's predecessor as program director.

Then there was a literature course surveying writers ranging from William Faulkner to Ed Abbey to Wendell Berry. It was taught by an irascible English professor whose advancing emphysema didn't stop him from smoking, backpacking, or from spending several months each year in India working in a Tibetan Buddhist colony.

Winter brought a forestry-school course on wilderness ecology taught by McQuillan. He was known to wear a tam-o'-shanter and employ his native Scots brogue in fireside renditions of Robert Burns poetry. There was also a humanities course on native American literature, a philosophy course called "Nature and Cosmology," and a drama course. Yes, drama, and it was every bit as odd as it sounds. This was the class that resulted in some students showing up naked, but, as it turned out, it was the course that knotted together the threads of this diverse academic weave.

Diversity is an important theme of the program, revealing its philosophical roots. In 1971 UM launched a venture that was to become the predecessor to Wilderness and Civilization, a program called the Round River Experiment. McQuillan says Round River was one of those quirky developments "that came out of the sixties' hippie movement."

But it also was a bit ahead of its time in that it was steeped in environmentalism. Its very name came from no less a figure than Aldo Leopold, whose essay *The Round River* made a case for a new sort of thinking drawn at "right angles to evolution."

"This calls for a reversal of specialization; instead of learning more and more about less and less, we must learn more about the whole biotic landscape," Leopold wrote. The plan was to ape the diversity of nature in academia.

Round River, which once involved 100 students, died, but its ethic survives in Wilderness and Civilization. Five of the professors involved in Round River teach the successor program. That legacy of diversity—to use a phrase in vogue, a holistic approach to the environment—forms the character of the current program. What's interesting, though, is how that diversity shapes the character of the students in Wilderness and Civilization. There were some curious developments.

For instance there was anger. The program draws its share of what we know as "funhogs," kids whose privileged rearing has allowed for a collection of skiing, windsurfing, and climbing gear, plus lingo such as "Gnarly," "Way cool," and "Awesome!" These are outdoor people whose time spent on ski slopes has deprived them of time to learn about the problems that threaten the outdoors they love.

Some of the program's classes, particularly the environmental science class, are designed to correct that naiveté. Ron Erickson, who holds a graduate degree in chemistry and has a background in philosophy, teaches that course by building a sobering case for the severity of the world's environmental problems. This comes as news to some funhogs. It's news they take hard, to the point of serious depression, says Jim Thormahlen, a teaching assistant. They're considering adding a counseling session to the curriculum to counteract depression.

But the more common reaction is activism, a development that McQuillan sees as no problem at all. Here, probably, is where the program takes its biggest chance by openly courting the wrath of the highly charged politics of the state. Montana is a timber state where designation of wilderness areas is viewed as lost timber jobs. That view foments a political battle with all the vehemence, if not quite the volume, of the spotted owl controversy in the Pacific Northwest.

Into this mix come 25 mostly out-of-state students with an inclination to do battle for wild lands. And they do. During the year, some students enlisted in *Earth First!* events and in grassroots groups that defend the wilderness. Marches were organized, banners hung, and the concept of ecotage or monkeywrenching lurked near the surface. On one field trip to a Bureau of Land Management office, some students left anti-BLM slogans scrawled on a blackboard. Some of the program's alumni have become full-time environmental activists. The state's Board of Regents balked at granting an accredited wilderness minor to graduates of the program, mostly because of the politically charged nature of the issue. (A wilderness minor for completion of the year-long program was recently approved by UM.)

McQuillan says he does not fear a political backlash will threaten the program's academic freedom. "If it did happen, it would either give the university the chance to show that it was independent and free-thinking, or it would show that the university was corrupt. And if it showed that the university was corrupt, that would be a change for the better. In my mind, it's not the job for the Wilderness and Civilization program to train activists, but at the same time, its not our job to suppress activists. If people have a tendency toward activism, it should be the job of the program to help them understand their feelings, and know some background about where their ideas come from and generally enhance their understanding, so if they are going to be activists then they can be better activists."

Activism is a part of what the program is about, a part that may even be seen as the whole by some students and even the politicians of the region. This misses the point, and the point may be subversive still, as subversive as backpacking itself can be.

This all came together for me one in day in science class when Erickson, the chemist-philosopher, was teaching about wilderness law with a Gary Snyder poem. (I told you the program was interdisciplinary.) Snyder makes the case not for wilderness in the land, but for designation and preservation of wilderness in every individual. The poem says:

I would like to say
Coyote is forever
Inside you
But it's not true.

What we do as backpackers is not merely recreation, or even about visiting wild places. It is rather about the preservation of the coyote that is in us all—about preserving the personal howl that the numbing forces of our society can silence. The art of cinching on a pack and setting off afoot is not mere sport. It is about the rediscovery of internal landscape mirroring the unfettered wild lands we stalk.

Usually such notions of personal liberation are not the business of academia as we have come to know it. Nonetheless, it is education in a pure form. McQuillan and the rest are running a subversive program. Traditional education is about shaping people to assume roles in society, whether those roles are in the corporations or in the arguably more rigid structure of academia itself. Traditional education is about taming people. UM's Wilderness and Civilization program is about keeping people wild, a role McQuillan explicitly acknowledges.

"That which is wild is self-willed. If we go imposing our will on it then it's not wild anymore," he says, speaking about both land and students. "Nobody can tell you what to think. Nobody should tell you what to think. That's one of the good things that has come out of 200 years of the age of reason."

Back to those naked people. Their state of undress was their own answer to an assignment to "do something outrageous." Randy Bolton, once chairman of the university's drama department, now taking more time to devote to his poetry and occasional shamanic journeys, frequently teaches with such assignments. He said he encourages students to show up nude or do anything else that presses the limits that society has placed on them.

"My goal is to try to guide that person to their internal wilderness, or a spontaneous place that is uninhibited," he said. That approach made his classes seethe with conflict, down to screaming matches with students directly challenging him. Bolton, whose bushy black beard and fringe of frizz around a bald head make him look like a troll, frequently was drenched in sweat from the emotional heat that would erupt.

"I'm not going to change that. I'm committed to that heat," he says. "I feel pretty good about that, that kind of controversy, that kind of conflict."

I finally got a chance to step back and consider all of this in mid-March. The students were scheduled to head 750 miles south of Montana's lingering winter for a two-week walk through the canyons, mesas, and slickrock plateaus of southeast Utah.

On a slickrock overlooking Arches National Park, you can be alone and lost in a place haunted by Edward Abbey. He wrote *Desert Solitaire* on this spot, and I wanted to come here to think not so much about wilderness as freedom, which is really what Abbey's best book is about. I'd driven here with Matt Colligen, another student in the program, a 20-year-old kid who'd left his native Michigan and at-best checkered academic career to figure out what he could about the pull of wild places. We had driven 12 straight hours out of Missoula. We landed in high desert about 1:00 a.m., in time to spread sleeping bags on slickrock under a full moon.

The sun blasted across the rock the next morning as I pumped the stove for coffee. Here was a place that defined the very concept of freedom and wildness. I sipped my coffee wondering whether this place, or all the reading and thinking the students had just done, could communicate that notion to these kids.

Then Matt rolled out of his sleeping bag. He didn't even say much, didn't even bother with coffee. He just stared off across the sweep of sandstone that stretched clear to the sun, and he grinned. It takes a quirky psyche to smile at a vast desert bitten by a bitter March wind. It was unmarked land, that foreboding space that some elements of our society seek to subdue.

Matt's grin broadened with the sun, and he headed away from the road. "I think I'll go get lost," he said. And he did. There may be something to this notion of education after all.

Adapted (with permission) from an article by Richard Manning first published in Backpacker *Magazine.*

Olympic Wilderness Classroom

Olympic Park Institute

It's six a.m., a Saturday in August, at a rain- spattered beach near Portage Head on the Olympic seashore. Sixteen bundled-up, booted men and women slog across the beach toward the rocky tideline, peering into pools.

Seagulls hover, perhaps suspecting us of competing for their customary breakfast fare. Not to worry, gulls. We'll leave everything as we found it. For we are here to acquire knowledge and understanding, not clams and mussels.

We are an Olympic Park Institute class on Life at the Ocean's Edge, led by Dr. Ladd Johnson of Stanford University. We are here at this ungodly hour because it's low tide, the best time to observe sea stars, anemones, kelp, algae and all the other inhabitants of this damp, complex world that joins land and sea. Before we're through with the three-day field seminar, we'll be more familiar with and respectful toward the life-styles and interrelationships of all these organisms. In the words of Jeff Carter, program director of the institute, we'll be more environmentally literate.

The Olympic Park Institute is a private, nonprofit organization that conducts environmental education courses with the entire Olympic Peninsula as its outdoor classroom. Participants include schoolchildren and Elderhostelers, as well as those in the field seminars. OPI is headquartered at historic Rosemary Inn on Lake Crescent, where modern concepts of hands-on, eyes-on, ears-on education mingle with authentic rusticity of yesteryear.

Rosemary's story goes back 75 years. In 1914, when tourism was lower-key and the charms of the Olympic Peninsula were just being discovered, Rose Littleton created a self-sufficient wilderness resort with a rambling central lodge, 18 cottages scattered over the lawn, a pier, a windmill to pump water from the lake, tennis courts, croquet, safe swimming for children, and rowboats for fishing. Rosemary Inn (named for Rose Littleton and her longtime assistant, Mary Daum) flourished until the 1930s.

Now, after four decades of near abandonment to the elements (marginal maintenance kept the roof from leaking), Rosemary still looks much as it did. This is thanks to a partnership between Olympic National Park and the Olympic Park Institute. The park is in charge of physical restoration of the old cabins and the grounds; OPI has built new housing, is restoring the lodge, and runs the programs.

Far-Flung Field Seminars

OPI grew out of the Olympic Field Seminar program, initiated by Jerry Edelbrock in 1984. As director of outdoor education for the Park, Edelbrock put together a summer-long series of field trips, mostly on weekends. Highly qualified instructors led groups of up to 15 to the beaches, mountains, river valleys, and every corner of the park. Participants brought their own camping equipment and food and carpooled from campground to destination. Some were teachers, taking the course for credit. All had in common a curiosity and concern about the outdoors.

By 1987 the field seminars offered under the umbrella of Olympic Park Institute had become independent of the Park. The array of courses had grown to nearly 30, including that Ocean's Edge seminar I attended. Some took place well outside Olympic National Park.

In 1986, for example, a class ventured to the slopes of Mt. St. Helens to check on the return of life six years after the big blast—and to monitor current tremblings through a portable seismometer. The search for life was rewarded, even on the great rockstrewn plain over which the crater's maw yawned. A trickle of meltwater ran down the baking desert slope, and where it formed a little pool, grasses and tiny trees were taking hold. Despite the instructor's assurance that this was to be expected in the natural course of the devastated area's recovery, we could not regard it as anything but a small miracle.

Currently the seminar program has retreated to its home base, Olympic National Park. Among the choices in a recent catalog were seminars on flowers, butterflies, birds, mosses, mushrooms, tidepool creatures, archaeological sites, and pioneer homes and routes. Nothing on the Olympic Peninsula is alien to OPI.

One course identifies plants used by native peoples, sending graduates home determined to add sorrel to their salads, nettles to their soups, and yerba buena to their teapots.

Another, perennially popular, explores the Hoh Valley haunts of the Roosevelt elk. Nobody ever forgets the sight of these majestic creatures filing through a forest glade, antlers aloft, masters of the rain forest. Or the sound of the bull elk's piercing, high-pitched bugle call, as he rounds up his harem.

In others, just as stimulating but less strenuous, students may learn how to make a cedar basket, photograph a petroglyph, paint a seastack's portrait, or write an ode to a cedar.

At the end of the day the student returns to Rosemary Inn for dinner, perhaps a stroll by the lake, perhaps a slide lecture or discussion, then tumbles early into a bunk bed.

Every year brings something new. In 1990, for example, one class reexplored Puget Sound in the style of Peter Puget and the Wilkes Expedition. Students sailed in two reconstructed boats built by the Puget Sound Society.

Another class will offer storytelling workshops, with assistance from a Native American teacher. Full details on all classes are in catalogs available from OPI.

The Way It Was

In the past everyone lodged in new dorm-style cabins, but a number of the old cabins are now in working order. Each of these storybook dwellings is different, from a log cabin with wooden hinges, to a shingled cottage with diamond-pane windows. Their builder was John Daum—Mary Daum's brother—an inventive man who was given free rein in design and construction. Restoring his often quirky architecture has become a cause for the National Park Service, which takes history very seriously. Everything must be just as it was, down to the old names (like Dardanella, Dreamerie, Alabam). They are true to color too. Dave Colthorp, a skilled builder and restorer, has scraped through layers of paint to find the originals. When a modern visitor looks askance at the garish red and green of Alabam, Colthorp grins and says, "Well, that's the way it was in 1925."

The weathered, shingled lodge, too, looks much as it did. Its rambling, rustic style is similar to that of Lake Crescent Lodge, its neighbor down the lake. But Rosemary has its idiosyncrasies. One dormer is still clad in durable old cedarbark siding, and peeled logs serve as porch pillars. Inside are conference rooms upstairs and down, kitchens, and a big informal dining room with million-dollar views.

Would Rose Littleton approve of all this restoration and education at her inn? Very likely. Her aim was to create a family-oriented retreat, and she invited young and old to come to Rosemary and get away from it all. That's still part of the idea, but OPI goes a giant step beyond. As Jeff Carter emphasizes, "We're here to give people the knowledge and background they'll need to make thoughtful decisions. By education and frequent immersion in the unspoiled outdoors, we may develop the wisdom and respect required to save our planet."

A lofty goal—but if people like OPI and its participants don't aim for it, who will?

Adapted (with permission) from an article by Rachel Bard first published in Peninsula *magazine.*

Beneath Sun and Stars, Campers Learn the Tools of Activism

The National Audubon Society

Activists are not only answering the call of the wild when they attend an Audubon camp—they're responding to a summons for political action.

The National Audubon Society runs three summer camps for adults, two in the East and one in the West. The Audubon camps are renowned for the quality of the educational experience they offer. Countless professional and amateur naturalists and teachers got their start at an Audubon camp.

But after attending two camps last summer as a visiting staff member—to teach a short course in environmental activism—I was left with the understanding that campers come not only to ogle nature, but also to learn more about the wild world they're trying to protect. They're girding themselves for future battles back home.

Playing Roles in Plain Air

The Audubon camp in the West, nestled in a valley beneath the imposing peak of Whiskey Mountain in Wyoming, is a place where campers experience a little piece of heaven—and learn something along the way. The core of the camp program centers on natural history: geology, plant ecology, and birds. Camp Director Peg Abbott gets the most out of the mountain setting, imbuing her charges with her rich knowledge of the alpine ecosystem.

She has a multitalented staff to work with, among them Don Burgess. An ornithologist by trade, Burgess excels as a mock member of Congress, a fact I quickly discovered when I began my first activist session.

While half the campers traipsed off to help with field research, the other 20 sat before me with glazed looks in their eyes. Ready for hiking and a close look at the area's wildlife and plant life, they were perhaps a little disappointed at having to spend part of their time in my activist workshop. The mountains beckoned.

As part of the workshop, the group put together arguments for legislation to save ancient forests. Then came Don's shining moment, as he took up the role of "Congressman Blowhard" and ambushed the group with arguments against ancient forest protection. Unfazed, the "citizens" countered with arguments about the forest's unique ecosystem and rich biodiversity. They also talked economics. I was impressed.

The next day the other half took its turn. I called on Don again, and by now he had refined his assumed obtuseness on ancient forest ecology to high art. The second group proved as persuasive as the first. Both made a strong case for old trees: the activists were now ready to do a similar job on their legislators back home.

In the end, campers were armed with new ideas and tools for taking action to protect the natural world. And the word "activist" had taken on new dimensions. To Margaret Mulvey from North Carolina, it now meant speaking your mind on things you care about. "You know," she said, "the word used to have some negative connotations for me. But I see it differently now."

Island Inspiration

The Audubon camp on Hog Island, off the rocky coast of Maine, is a world of spruce and moss, foggy mornings, and charming New England buildings (to house campers and staff). It also has some fine hospitality to offer. Bob Dorrance, camp director, greets the new campers and helps them feel comfortable on their island home. Boat trips regularly leave for other islands, offering study of their flora and fauna. One island in route supports a nesting pair of bald eagles and their young.

Inspiration always visits the Audubon camps. The joy of learning is apparent on every face, and the teachers, many of them old hands, know how to involve everyone. Nevertheless, it is a challenge getting people excited about what goes on in the halls of Congress after they've spent a day witnessing the wonders of marine life.

During my workshops on the "Ecology of Congress," though, the campers were enthusiastic and sharp. Like their Western counterparts, they recognized that studying nature is fun, but protecting it is equally important. They took what I had to offer and asked for more. For the rest of the week, I was besieged by advice-seekers.

"I teach seventh graders and I've thought about having them write their congressman," said one camper. "Do you think that's a good idea?" Not good, great! But I offered this advice to increase effectiveness: Send the letters in one packet, with a cover letter asking for just one reply rather than individual replies. It may improve the chances of getting a response.

The two camps helped me to be a better teacher. They're set up to help teachers teach. They enrich the lives of everyone. The camp programs are more than just a close look at another pretty face of nature; that rare species called activism is also carefully studied and keenly sought among the rocks, the waterfalls, and the quiet trails shared with a myriad of wildlife.

Adapted (with permission) from an article by Connie Mahan first published in Audubon Activist.

Fiji

Project Ocean Search

"Let's design for the future rather than be victims of it."

So concluded Cousteau Society ecologist Dr. Richard Murphy, speaking to 35 people from 23 states and three countries. They sat in a circle on a beach on Vanau Levu, Fiji's second largest of 322 islands. These jet-lagged travelers were the beginning of Project Ocean Search. This Cousteau program has taken place for the past 19 years in a variety of locations and returns to Fiji each summer.

That first night a reasonable question was, "What do a shrimp-boat builder, television journalist, dentist, professional windsurfer, graduate student, and housewife have in common?" A fascination with the ocean was the initial answer; but for the next two weeks, this diverse group would discover other bonds that connect them with each other and the larger world. They would experience a tropical reef system and meet people from an island culture that is still intact but struggling to maintain harmony with the surrounding natural environment. They would share thoughts on the puzzle of how to live peacefully on an overwhelmed planet.

Traditionally, Project Ocean Search (POS) is located on an island removed from the pressures of urban civilization, where people can reconnect to a healthy environment that inspires a concern to protect and preserve. Open to anyone over age 16, POS is based on a belief that a deep understanding of nature and the value of natural resources can best come from personal experience. Although not an expedition on *Calypso of Alcyone*, POS simulates the vigorous activity and inquiry of a full-scale Cousteau expedition.

Daily scuba dives focus on different aspects of natural history, including how animals adapt to their environment and meet the needs of survival. In addition, participants explore the island with experienced naturalists, work with biologists to learn about research techniques, learn underwater photography, or find a deserted beach and discuss literature of the sea.

Afternoon lectures focus on coral reef ecology, resource management, invertebrate and fish ecology, marine mammals, marine archaeology, humanities of the sea, history of diving, and updates on current Cousteau Society expeditions by expedition crew members. In the evening, visiting lecturers share their knowledge of Fiji and its people, or Cousteau staff members present films and slides on a variety of topics focusing on humankind's relationship to the environment.

In a day's time, participants may dive with lionfish, a sea snake, and butterflyfish, then surface to a talk about where and how such creatures fit into the dynamic reef ecosystem as evolved residents. After lunch, the group may board an island bus and travel beneath tall coconut trees to one of the nearby Fijian villages where they are welcomed by a traditional yaqona, or kava ceremony. Passing a cup of murky liquid, village chieftains welcome visitors by inviting them to sip from a coconut shell. In the village, everything is shared.

In a country where 87 percent of the land is still owned by local people, there is strong interest in preservation. The price to be paid for developing slowly may be that the average income per capita is still only $2,000, but it quickly becomes obvious that such standard economics don't fully describe the quality of life here, where no one goes hungry and nearly every view presents an abundance of vegetation or blue sea.

Speaking to the villagers, Jean-Michel Cousteau explains, "We believe it is important to people from Western cultures to see how a person can have a high quality of life in an environment where the forests and reefs have not been destroyed and where traditional values give people a sense of belonging. We believe Fijians demonstrate this as well as any culture on the planet."

In a world increasingly held hostage by petroleum supplies, military dangers, and population pressures, it is perhaps not a luxury to travel so far to contemplate global and individual problems. Such serious concerns may best be investigated against the backdrop of a quiet Fijian Bay fringed by hazy mountains, high white clouds, and palm trees, where coralline rocks, wiggling with life, protrude at low tide, exposing sea cucumbers and blue starfish, or where a shell scurries, propelled tanklike by a hermit crab, and where a smiling Fijian woman wades at low tide and calls, "Bula, bula," hello in Fijian. It makes the future look more inviting.

Adapted (with permission) from an article by Pam Stacey first published in Calypso Log.

The AWLS Experience

![divider line]

The American Wilderness Leadership School
Safari Club International

Most hunters and sportsmen are probably familiar with Safari Club International. This group of men and women are dedicated conservationists and comprise the most active hunting organization in the world. Conservation of wildlife and protection of the hunter is their motto, and they also emphasize responsible hunting. The worldwide organization has many worthwhile goals and objectives, some of which include promoting conservation of the world's renewable wildlife resources, recognizing hunting as one of the many management tools, and educating our youth about the outdoors and natural resources.

Back in 1973, SCI founded their Conservation Fund to preserve floundering conservation education programs initiated by government agencies. In 1976, the Conservation Fund was responsible for developing the American Wilderness Leadership School (AWLS) to reach students and teachers with the message that wise use of natural resources is vital to the future of our country. What better way to reach our younger generation than through educated teachers?

The Granite Ranch was then purchased in 1982. This magnificent piece of property is situated in the foothills of the Gros Ventre Wilderness area of the Bridger-Teton National Forest, 36 miles southeast of Jackson Hole, Wyoming. The ranch is surrounded by breathtaking natural beauty and contains all the elements essential to studying environmental issues. Since purchasing this 34-acre property, SCI members and chapters have raised money to construct a western-style lodge, which provides dining and classroom facilities, along with a library and second-floor lodging.

The objective of the Conservation Fund and AWLS is to offer an outdoor instructional program that concentrates on natural resource management and provides participants with the knowledge necessary to better comprehend and evaluate today's conservation and ecology issues. I guess that could be simplified by saying the AWLS program is an academic course in nature.

The program consists of two separate sessions. First of all, high-school students sponsored by SCI's many chapters come from all over the world. This age group was chosen in order to expose students to conservation or related career opportunities at a time when these options are being considered. Also, young adults in this age group are becoming active in school and community activities as informed citizens. Programmed and well-planned experiences both in the classroom and on field trips into the surrounding parks and wilderness areas emphasize the understanding of natural resources.

In the second session, teachers and administrators take part in the 10-day program. Teachers experience the same activities and instruction as the students, but they also receive ideas for implementing conservation education programs in their schools.

Teachers are also provided with follow-up assistance and materials for conducting student and teacher workshops in their local districts.

Participants who encounter the AWLS experience face challenging times in the fields of wildlife management, ecology, conservation, hunter safety, fishing, wilderness survival, shooting sports, backpacking, white-water rafting, and outdoor ethics.

I was fortunate enough to be a participant in the teacher and administrator session this past summer. Ten days in the Wyoming Rockies tying flies, catching trout, shooting trap, learning to use a compass, taking field trips to state and federal management areas, and making new friends is not a bad way to spend part of a summer vacation. My class was made up of teachers and administrators representing 12 different states ranging from California to Florida and many places in between. Some were hunters, many were not. Even a few antihunters were present in this diverse group.

Our first day consisted of registration, room assignments, orientation, and getting-acquainted sessions. But on the second day the program got rolling with a shooting sports session that lasted all afternoon. First we attended an informative discourse on range safety and basic gun-handling skills. Then we rotated among three activities: blackpowder, handgun, and rifle, with trapshooting for everyone. A few of the participants had never fired a gun before, but everyone had an enjoyable afternoon. Safety instructions and general information regarding firearms was well received, and the hands-on experience was a benefit to everyone. Several members of the class admitted they didn't realize how much fun the shooting sports could be.

The next morning Gene Decker from Colorado State University lectured on wildlife ecology and conservation. Emphasis was placed on wildlife management and the positive and negative role that society had played. Later in the afternoon we rotated between fly-tying, map and compass reading, and Granite Creek flora. I hadn't tied flies since I was a kid and did it ever show. Some of the participants were so talented that they could probably pick up a few extra bucks selling flies to trout fishermen. Forest Buchanan, an authority on plants and flowers as well as the official AWLS naturalist, entertained the group with his vast knowledge about plant life. After supper, one of the ladies caught a nice cutthroat trout on a fly she tied in class.

Talk about a Happy Camper

Day four found us at a winter big-game feeding ground. Habits of elk and mule deer were discussed as well as feeding procedures. During our week-and-a-half trip we saw several head of elk, mule deer, antelope, moose, bison, and many other species of animal and bird life. Then the discussion turned to fish ecology. At a nearby creek we collected samples of aquatic life and even examined a few fish to determine age, health, and other important factors. Later in the day we saw the Jackson Elk Refuge and the Teton Park Interpretive Center, and we spent a few hours in Jackson Hole visiting the many shops and tourist gatherings. The busy academic schedule did not allow for a lot of free time, and the evening in Jackson Hole was a real treat.

The next day we all loaded up in the SCI school bus, the "Blue Goose," and drove to the Wildlife and Public Land Management Bureau. There we witnessed firsthand some of the important issues surrounding multiple-use land management. Afterward, we were off to the state fish hatchery for an informative lecture. In the afternoon, Joe Vogler, coordinator of Wyoming's Project Wild, entertained the group with ideas and games to be implemented in the classroom. Vogler was instrumental in developing the Project Wild program for elementary and secondary education that is now active in 49 states. Each day was filled with informative and educational sessions with innovative ideas enhancing old topics. Superintendents, principals, and teachers like me all learned from each other's experience. Personally, I was glad to see administrators attending the workshop. I feel this experience will give them a better understanding of the importance that environmental education plays in our society.

Later in the week we departed for Yellowstone National Park. Wildlife there was plentiful, and everyone could clearly see the new grass and plant life prospering after the massive fire that received so much media coverage. My folks had taken me to Yellowstone when I was about five years old, but I simply couldn't recall many things. I was impressed by the magnitude of the park's natural beauty. Harlen Kredit, a biology teacher from Washington state employed by SCI for 19 summers, gave us a special tour. Right before dark we set up tents, and I was thrilled that my two tent mates were experienced campers. Supper was cooked over an open flame, and lies were told until bedtime.

The next morning we drove around the park observing the many geographical features and taking pictures of elk and bison. Around noon we got to see Old Faithful in action, which drew a crowd of around 5,000 shutterbugs. It didn't seem as impressive as it did 29 years ago, but this wonder of nature still amazes me. Later in the evening, after returning to the lodge, about half of us headed for the hot springs located within a mile of the school. Don't get me wrong, sleeping on the ground at Yellowstone was great, but after 30 minutes in the 98 degree water, most of us were ready for a nice bed with a good mattress.

Our last full day at Granite Creek was full of nail-biting suspense as we experienced the white-water raft trip down the Snake River. The eight-mile float was scenic and packed with adventure. It was most definitely a climactic end to a fabulous 10-day outdoor experience. Our evening was filled with a group picture, cookout, and tomahawk throwing championship. My team lost, and lacking good sportsmanship, I vowed never to throw another hatchet as long as I live. Truthfully, it was a lot of fun and during graduation that night, most of us hated to see it end. Something special happened during those 10 days.

As we left for the airport the next morning, we witnessed first-hand the predator/prey relationship that had been discussed during one of our lectures. A coyote chased and caught a young fawn mule deer directly across from the lodge. It was an awesome sight indeed, one that many people fail to understand, but nevertheless it happens in the real world. Wildlife abounds on Granite Creek; we saw mule deer and moose feeding almost everyday near the lodge. Somebody knew what they were doing when this piece of property was purchased.

Adapted (with permission) from an article by Mark Hampton first published in Petersen's Hunting.

Amazon Adventure

Amazonia Expeditions

August 11, 1989

Hi, Guys!

The witch doctor who's been treating me said to stay off the leg for a while, so I thought I'd zip off a few postcards. Less than a week into this gig and so far I've slogged through the densest jungle you can imagine, fallen out of a canoe into piranha-infested water with a crocodile in my hand, chased snakes, and had an unidentified foot-long millipede crawl around on my neck. Guess it's what you'd call your typical Amazon vacation. Who knows, maybe I'll get seduced by a mermaid before it's over.

Keep one cold for me,

Jeff

During my first trip to Peru in 1989, when that postcard was written, I learned that the natives deep in the Amazon jungle believe in blonde, blue-eyed mermaids. They also believe the pink dolphins living in their rivers metamorphose into handsome young men for the purpose of seducing the village maidens, and that you can become possessed by demons, bringing you bad luck, a host of maladies, and making you do a variety of things against your will.

Most of my friends believe demonic possession is the only explanation for my behavior.

Telling them I was returning to the Peruvian rain forest, arguably the best tropical rain forest in the world, for a couple of weeks and taking my wife Mary along elicited one of two distinct reactions—either their eyes lit up with feigned excitement or they looked at me as though I was croaking in an unintelligible, alien tongue.

Then the inevitable: *Why?*

Telling them it was because Mary didn't think I'd done an adequate job of souvenir acquisition last year wasn't convincing. Explaining that we were going to fish, swim, explore, canoe, and fight off mosquitoes didn't seem to justify the perceived risk either—we could do all that without leaving Iowa.

Traveling to the Amazon meant—what?—we were going to get eaten by a mindless school of blood-frenzied piranha, shredded by a 12-foot crocodile, or crushed into silly putty by a 30-foot anaconda.

On June 22, the day before our departure, we got together with some friends for a send-off of sorts—it disturbed Mary when they all said good-bye as though we'd never return.

Both the expedition I'd been on in 1989 and the one we went on in 1990 were led and organized by Paul Beaver, the head honcho of Amazonia Expeditions Inc. of Gainesville, Florida. Paul received a Ph.D. in an esoteric jungle animal science from the University of Chicago before deciding that leading *tourists*, as he calls us, into the jungle was more interesting. With that in mind he formed an expeditionary company about 10 years ago based on the apparently unique concept of individual attention. The groups he takes down usually number between 10 and 15 tourists with an equally large staff of expert jungle guides, cooks, and helpers.

Phil was happy to hear I was returning and thrilled to learn Mary was joining me. "We've seen so many neat things lately," he said when I called to confirm the dates. The itinerary Paul presented for the two-week expedition sounded simple enough, beginning with two easy days of jungle acclimation and continuing from there with increasingly varied activities to choose from, ending with what he called a "rafting experience" for those whose thrill quota still wasn't met after 10 days. That we'd see a lot of "neat things" was a clear case of understatement.

After flying into Iquitos, Peru, we boated for an hour up one of the Amazon's 1,100-odd tributaries to a nice, relatively luxurious lodge—later referred at as "The Amazon Hilton"—for our two-day acclimation with some mild jungle stuff.

Rare red uakari monkeys, saddleback marmosets, and a dozen different species of macaws and parrots, toucans and tanagers, and a bird-eating tarantula larger than Arachnaphobia's Big Bob were all encountered while thrashing around in the jungle during those easy days near the Hilton.

Early on the morning of our third day we loaded onto the Safari 1—a 1960s thatched-roof version of the *African Queen*—for a two-day ride upriver to our base camp built on the Yarapa near the headwaters of the Rio Amazonas.

For most of the next week we swam with the pink dolphins; fished for, caught, and ate piranha; helped catch a caiman one day and a three-toed sloth another; and chased a parrot snake away from the dock where we bathed in the river.

These are now referred to as Normal Jungle Activities. On the afternoon of the fourth day, we had our first Non-Normal Jungle Activity.

Five of us tourists—Jeanne, Alice, Mary, Wally, and I—along with Paul and Alejandro, his helper, were moseying back toward camp from a mild jungle walk where we'd gotten introduced to a wide variety of plant life—which ones to eat if you were bitten by a snake, which ones cured diarrhea, which vines and coconuts contained pure water, which ones would cause death in a minute if eaten—when Alejandro spotted a small group of pygmy marmosets, the world's smallest primate.

We observed each other for about 40 minutes. Paul's eyes were wide with excitement during the entire episode, claiming he saw 1,000 saddleback marmosets for every pygmy.

Before the marmosets tired of our comical squeaking and chattering attempts at drawing them closer, we decided to move on. Minutes later the midafternoon tranquility of the jungle was shattered with a sound I'd only heard during feeding time at the zoo's Big Cat House.

I hurried around a clump of underbrush toward the source of the commotion and found Alejandro 10 meters away, wide-eyed, pointing into the jungle and saying, "Otorongo! Otorongo!" You instinctively know that you've had a close encounter when the normally passive Indian's eyes are saucered with excitement.

Alejandro had startled a jaguar, which then bounded into the jungle, maybe three meters in front of him. "How big was it?" I asked through the roar—generated cacophony of squawking parrots and howling monkeys. He spread his arms to full width and said in Spanish, "150, maybe 200." I'd already begun thinking in meters rather than feet, but it still took a few moments before I realized that Alejandro's unit of measurement was kilograms.

We bunched into a tight pack and rapidly followed Alejandro back to camp that, we were somewhat disturbed to discover, was only 50 meters from the encounter site—a very short distance that most of us thought about that night.

Bright and early on the morning of the sixth day, five of us tourists—this time it was Jeanne, Jim, Bev, Mary, and I—left the fog-shrouded Varapa for a rugged one-day excursion with Paul's top two jungle studs, Jose Luis and Segundo. Supposedly, we were on a primer of sorts for a three-day "wilderness camping experience" that we thought sounded like fun.

Jose Luis is Amazonia Expeditions' Top Guide, and probably one of the best guides in the jungle for getting you there and back again. Segundo is the Top River and Jungle Man in the area—perhaps even better than Jose Luis. The difference between being a Top Guide and a Top Jungle Man is that guides speak English. Jose Luis taught himself and speaks almost fluently, especially now that we've taught him the proper idiomatic usage of such phrases as "happy campers" and "Are you having fun yet?"

Though we'd been in the jungle for nearly a week and had several pretty exciting adventures, this was the first time we'd gone out with Jose Luis and Segundo—which was seen as a mixed blessing of sorts. It was reassuring to know that the vastness of their combined expertise was available to keep us from killing ourselves.

It was disconcerting to realize that the vastness of the combined expertise might be needed.

Our goals for the day were two fairly remote lakes where hoatzins and monkeys are abundant. Monkeys are abundant almost everywhere in the jungle. But hoatzins—birds that stopped evolving just this side of their dinosaur ancestors about 100 million years ago—are fairly rare.

Within an hour it became apparent that Michael Douglas and Kathleen Turner were chopping their way through a banana farm when filming *Romancing the Stone*. We strolled with relative ease through one of those for a while before Segundo stopped, looked around for a moment, and abruptly led us off the path and into what we were certain was virgin jungle. Nothing resembled a path.

Segundo loped along out in front, his seldom-used machete cradled in his hand and knapsack with our lunch slung over his shoulder, followed by Jose Luis who slashed away at the ubiquitous vines with his machete for the tourists' benefit.

Toward 11 a.m. we arrived at the first lake drenched in sweat and tired—except, of course, Jose Luis and Segundo, who still looked as fresh and calm as they had when we'd left base camp. Segundo faded into the jungle while the rest of us took what we considered as a well-earned break. I mentioned to Jose Luis that I'd feel better if he and Segundo would sweat a little every now and then, especially since Segundo was wearing a long-sleeved shirt. Jose Luis laughed and said that jungle men don't sweat.

Segundo returned from his scouting mission and reported that he'd seen a flock of hoatzins on the lake shore. We groaned and moved on.

There they were, a dozen or so of the prehistoric fowl perched in trees along the lake shore looking like punk turkeys with spiked crests. As we watched them, several squirrel monkeys were watching us, undetected until Segundo pointed them out.

The second lake, an hour further inland, proved impossible to reach—the water was too high, the marshy jungle growth too dense. Just as well, perhaps, breakfast had worn off before reaching the last lake. We found a small clearing, spread a couple of ponchos and redistributed Segundo's load by eating lunch.

About the time a siesta began sounding like a good idea, Segundo, who'd been attentive as a hawk the whole time, indicated we should start heading back.

Less than 10 minutes into our return trek, as we approached a log bridge over a small, clear-water stream, Segundo held up his hand to halt us. He crept toward the stream's bank, pointed to the ground and said a word I'd heard two days earlier—Otorongo.

Five large jaguar prints, prints that weren't there when we crossed the log an hour earlier, were embedded in the wet clay bank just off the log, and headed in the direction of our recent camp site.

Jose Luis and Segundo whispered a bit in Spanish, then Jose Luis said it was time to start moving again. We crossed the stream and headed off along a muddy jungle path at a substantially increased pace.

Segundo pointed around and mentioned something to Jose Luis. I asked for a translation. "Segundo says we are in the jaguar's living room." A superfluous verification: it was apparent—mostly because of the trampled underbrush and abundance of small skeletons—that something that large considered the neighborhood its home.

Two hours later we regained the trail through the banana farm, and I noticed with mild pleasure that Jose Luis' T-shirt was damp with perspiration.

The morning of the tenth day found us six hours upriver on a very minor, very wild tributary called the Pumayaco, having been transported by *El Terrible*, Segundo's homemade motorboat. Pumayaco, by the way, means "jaguar urine" in the local language—a bit of jungle trivia we weren't let in on until after we'd gotten there.

Not that it would have made any difference. By then we'd had at least one more close encounter of the jaguar kind, gotten within arms reach of an anaconda large enough to make quality zoos jealous, fought off multitudes of assassin bugs from Planet Neptune, and crossed so many slime-covered, backwater, electric-eel breeding pools and streams on fallen log bridges that, like someone who'd had too much to drink, we'd begun to suffer from impaired judgment.

Jeanne, Wally, Mary, and I, along with Jose Luis and Top Apprentice Guide, Clider, walked away from the camp's relative comfort and security and our fellow wilderness campers, to enjoy a "rafting experience."

For the next five hours, Jose Luis and Clider slashed a path through virgin jungle with the machetes until we regained the Pumayacu well upstream of the wilderness camp.

Construction of the raft was begun under a blue sky and completed in a torrential downpour that pushed Mary's and Jeanne's resolve to the edge. Standing ankle-deep in mud on the edge of the quicksand pit Mary had accidentally discovered earlier in the afternoon, Jeanne implored Jose Luis to abandon the raft building and lead us, or at least her and Mary, back to the presumably dry safety of the wilderness camp.

It was near violation of our only rule: No Whining.

In contrast, Mary, who was clearly regretting her pre-trip resolution to always do whatever I did, had given herself up for dead earlier in the day and was observing the raft building with the mute resignation that it was the Amazonian equivalent of an Egyptian funeral barge, perhaps wishing we had a priest along to administer Last Rites.

Jose Luis sensed the tension and tested his understanding of the idioms he'd been learning, "are we having fun yet?" I thought he'd demonstrated nearly perfect inflection and situational usage. Jeanne's glare indicated that she didn't.

Jose Luis recovered, saying he couldn't lead them back—there wasn't enough daylight left. Besides, "Segundo has already cut down the trees."

The completed raft was five large logs wide, cross-braced and lashed together with a couple 100 meters of vine. It was huge by local standards, more massive than any Jose Luis or Segundo had built before.

As an act of appeasement to Jeanne and Mary, and because the raft-building site was too muddy to camp on, we christened our half-ton creation the *Titanic*, loaded on our gear, and headed downstream with about two hours of daylight remaining.

Jose Luis, Segundo, Wally, and I balanced on the *Titanic*'s corners, hefting long, forked poles to fend off the continuous tangle of logs, trees, and vines that obscured clear passage. Clider squatted on the front, clutching his machete. Mary and Jeanne rode in the middle, queens of the Pumayaco, clinging to false hopes of making it back to the wilderness camp before dark.

For the next hour we fought our way over and under partially submerged logs, got swept into the river by snarled vines and branches, and shooshed off the omnipresent ants and hand-sized spiders that dropped into the raft every few minutes.

"Jose Luis," Jeanne asked after scootching another one away, "are these spiders poisonous?"

Jose Luis looked at her as though she'd asked if the earth was round. "All spiders are poisonous," and with a sly grin, "how do you think they kill their prey?"

"They almost look like tarantulas."

"That is because they are."

A moment later I plucked one the size of a small plate off Mary's back—"Is this what you're talking about?"—and flipped it into the river.

For a moment my thoughts drifted back five days to the swampy edge of that remote lake we couldn't reach. After our picnic lunch I'd asked Jose Luis why we weren't seeing more snakes—I knew they were out there. Was it excellent camouflage? "For 200 meters," he said, sweeping his arm across the marshy vista in front of us, "I cannot imagine how many snakes are out there—boa, anaconda, fer-de-lance, coral . . . ." On the *Titanic* no one mentioned the snakes we weren't seeing.

With less than an hour of daylight left, we rounded a bend and came upon a sandy beach below the dense jungle. Segundo said it looked like a nice spot to camp. Jeanne, certain the wilderness camp couldn't be too much farther, protested. Rafting on the river "gets even more haunting at night," Jose Luis said, then, euphemistically, "even more fun." A convincing argument.

We prepared a small clearing and pitched our mosquito nets over some palm fronds we'd laid on the ground as moisture barriers. Clider gathered some dead wood and went to work trying to start a fire, a task he accomplished only with the aid of some kerosene.

Huddled around Clider's fire we determined that the major distinction between our gig and the "Jungle Survival Training" Paul offers were the cold canned sardines we'd had for supper and the bottle of tequila-like substance called Pisco that Jose Luis had magically produced from his knapsack.

We passed the bottle around until it was two-thirds empty and were feeling good about our prospects when Jose Luis said we needed to douse the fire before turning in. "There are vipers in the jungle that are attracted to heat."

The next morning we drank the last of the fresh water we'd carried in, boiled some river water for coffee and canteens, killed the rest of the Pisco, and cast off shortly after dawn.

A lottery was started on what time we'd get back to the wilderness camp. When we asked Jose Luis for his opinion, he hesitated a moment, casually punted his corner of the raft off another log, looked around and said, "I think I would like to see something I recognize before I say."

A bit disturbing.

"Uh-huh, how about Segundo?" Jose Luis asked.

More silence, then "Segundo also wants to recognize something first," Jose Luis translated.

"Jose Luis, have either of you ever been this far up the Pumayacu before?"

He studied the stream's banks and trees again. "I don't think so."

Another lottery was started on what day we'd get back.

A score of log barriers, two dozen tarantulas, and several million ants later, Segundo, who generally spoke only when asked something specific, volunteered something to Jose Luis. It seemed like a significant event, so I asked Jose Luis what he'd said.

"Segundo says that if there is a small blackwater stream coming in on the right around the next bend that he thinks he knows where we are."

Wally, who'd already perfected the technique of following his pole off the front of the raft in pursuit of a log, nearly executed another half gainer when we spotted a smallish blackwater stream in the neighborhood of where we hoped one would be.

Jeanne was the most excited on the crew—since it was just a little after nine in the morning, she figured her 10:30 guess was a lottery winner.

I won. Shortly before noon of the eleventh day, after forcing the *Titanic* under yet another log, we rounded a bend and saw *El Terrible* and Roy, an apprentice guide who'd been left behind by the rest of our "wilderness group" to wait for us.

We shouted our greetings of relief and a request, which sent him scrambling for a cold beer. Civilization!

You could see it in her eyes—the last thing the Miami customs agent wanted was a reason to inspect the clay encrusted duffels and backpacks, reeking of the Amazonian jungle, sitting on the floor in front of her.

She read our declaration card and glanced at the bags. "Been backpacking in Peru?"

"When we weren't canoeing or rafting, yeah."

"Bring back any plants? Animals? Liquor?" she dutifully asked. No. No. No.

I lied. A major portion of the stench surrounding us came from one of my backpacks where a bottle of a concoction based on the 150 proof sugar cane rum distilled deep in the jungle called Chuchuhuasi was slowing dissolving its cork. I was prepared to tell her it was an Amazonian aphrodisiac, but she didn't want to know.

"Please exit through the door over there," she said, hurriedly initialing our form.

Sure, Mary and I were simply returning from a two-week gig of backpacking, canoeing, and rafting in the Peruvian Amazon—an accurate, understated deception.

Adapted (with permission) from an article by Jeff McKinney first published in Amazonia Expeditions.

Encounter with Macaws

Amazonia Expeditions

It was five a.m., absolutely pitch black, and deep in the Amazon rain forest. My senses immediately came alive as the word "Guacamayo" was whispered outside my mosquito netting. Hastily I fumbled my way out of bed, stuck my legs in my jeans, pulled on my boots, and prayed that Wilson in the kitchen was up and had hot water for coffee. He did. I picked my way carefully down the muddy riverbank to the boat with my camera around my neck, flashlight between my teeth, canteen in one hand and coffee in the other. I settled down on a plank seat and whispered soft good mornings to my companions so as not to waken the sleeping camp above.

As we motored down the Yarapa toward our destination, my mind raced back and forth, up and down. Will they come this morning? Is it going to rain? Will we be there in time? Day is just starting to break and with it come all the sounds of the birds and small animals greeting the new day, but I was only momentarily diverted from my goal and looked around impatiently. I knew we were close. I'm sure that's the log I saw yesterday.

With some trepidation and a lot of help from Alejandro, Renee, and Paul, we ascended a 20-foot bank of mud and reached solid ground. Silently we marched a quarter of a mile deep into the jungle until we achieved our destination. Hardly discernible through the foliage was the tambo, a shelter built from palms, its purpose being to hide us—and hide it did. I knew if we hadn't had our jungle guides, we would have been aimlessly searching for hours for the blind.

Once inside the tambo, we quietly arranged our camera equipment, set our binoculars down, and waited. The jungle noises closed in on us, and I felt like we were really part of the jungle. The excitement and tension mounted. I asked what time it was often and was impatiently told that it was five minutes later than the last time I asked, so I shrugged my shoulders and told myself what will be, will be.

What's this? Renee was crouching and running toward the tambo, mouthing the words "Guacamayos!"—Macaws! I had to stop a minute and wipe my face—what a stupid time for my emotions to take hold. Click after click of the cameras. Look at them in the tree, jostling each other and flapping their wings, and all for the purpose of getting a taste of something out of that hole in the tree. Gorgeous chestnut-fronted macaws! What fun they were having just living and being. My word, I was thinking, there were at least 20. Wait now—a signal from the leader of the flock. And they were gone.

My heart was beating rapidly, and I was really having problems keeping my eyes clear. Twenty, 30 minutes passed—I was still in awe of what I had seen and was waiting again for the next extravaganza. While I strained to focus on and identify particular sounds coming out of the forest, the guides, being so attuned to their environment, recognized them long before we did. But then I heard them—wing beats, literally drowning out any other sound—red bellied macaws, right to that same hole in the tree. It must be 25 to 30 feet above the ground. Look at that! He pulled her tail to get a turn at the hole. I saw 12, no, maybe 15 macaws. Whatever is in that tree must be great. Once again, a signal and the flock left. No one in the tambo said a word. All I could do was smile. I couldn't help myself—the smile came from within.

A shorter wait this time. Once again I checked and rechecked my camera. Alejandro tip-toed up to the blind, his fingers to his lips—shshsh. No rush-approach to the tree this time but a cautious squawk right above our heads—I was afraid to move! I looked up to see, in all their red and yellow glory, scarlet macaws! I was clicking the camera so fast and breathing in short gasps. What a fabulous sight. I took the camera away from my face and just looked. My neck was starting to cramp and my arms were so tired from holding up that camera, but who cared? I was trying so hard to imprint this moment in my mind so I could recall it at will when I got home.

On our final day in the jungle, one of our guides, Segundo, climbed up that tree, using only vines as aids, to within a few feet of the hole where the macaws had congregated. He was able to scrape some of the dripping liquid and bark into an empty film container for me. That substance is now at Louisiana State University being analyzed by Dr. Thomas Tully, along with six different species of indigenous palm nuts that macaws are known to eat.

Compiling this information and other data that I've gathered from my trips with Paul in 1989 and 1990 is an exciting step forward toward the enhancement of husbandry and improved care in my captive macaw breeding program at home. Thanks to Paul and Milly, I have had the opportunity to expand my experience from working with captive birds to the observation of macaws in their natural environment.

Adapted (with permission) from an article by Leigh Ann Stennett first published in Amazonia Expeditions.

Transit to a Lost World

Ocean Voyages

Ancient mariners no doubt encountered by chance this tiny igneous speck in the Pacific vastness. But now, two days out of Puntarenas, we knew our schooner *Victoria* was closing in on Isla del Coco when her Swedish crew abandoned their pre-dinner chores and started pacing the decks. The taciturn navigator Leif Fahlgren stopped whisking the béarnaise and made his way forward. Christer, Lars, Bjorn, and Gunnar stopped peeling the potatoes and assembled with Leif near the foremast, each squinting sunward over the bowsprit. Kevin Burke, a Yorkshire Bermudian via Galway, wandered from the galley where the filets were thawing to join his Swedish comrades. Leif looked at his watch, stretched out his hand and as if by command, Cocos materialized—a gray, misty smudge slowly gaining definition on the limitless horizon.

At the same time, our collective image of Cocos was replaced by this more distinct reality. I, for one, had expected a dark cloud poised over a flame-racked volcano, pterodactyls soaring menacingly overhead. Instead, Isla del Coco—24 square kilometers of volcanic rock topped by rich vegetation and queer endemic species—perched on the horizon virtually unaltered since it first bubbled forth from the ocean bed.

Still, for a place that revealed no outward signs of change (for at least a millennium or two), Cocos has been shrouded by a fair bit of myth and mystery. There are many apparently credible tales of lost treasure. One hundred million dollars in gold was reportedly spirited out of Lima in the late eighteenth century during the early stages of a popular uprising, and deposited in a hastily dug hole near Coco's Chatham Bay. The treasure has become the object of at least one well-known fable. It is said that one foggy night in Harry White's bar on the San Francisco waterfront, a man named Peg Leg Benton related this tale of lost riches to a young nineteenth-century writer named Robert Louis Stevenson.

It is also widely believed that Cocos served as a kind of repository for plunder taken by pirates like Benito Bonito, who roamed the western coasts of South and Central America. And Cocos has a permanent diary of its less notorious visitors. Sailors off ships that have passed its way—"to take on sweet water and to make no economies of the coconuts"—have left the names of their vessels chiseled in stone near Chatham Bay.

All of this contributes to the aura of mystery that clings to Cocos, enhanced by the fierce Pacific currents that swirl around the craggy perimeter: the giant fish, the varieties of shark, the sinewy water-falls that cascade from the mountains meter after meter. There is a magic here, produced by the perpetual engine of nature unleashed, far from human failings and interference.

So how do you get to this strange place? There are two ways. You can volunteer to serve as one of the island's three guards. The Costa Rican Park Service will bring you out the roughly 275 miles from Puntarenas on a small coastal patrol vessel. (If they can find the island; one time they groped through the mist for nearly a week before making a hapless return to Puntarenas.) They'll deposit you in a tin hut at Wafer Bay that comes equipped with beans, rice, a balky generator, and an old Garand rifle, surplus from the Battle of the Marne.

Or, you can sign up aboard with Ocean Voyages, a Sausalito, California, charter firm that specializes in far-flung adventure cruising around the globe. Our trek to Cocos was only one of many exotic excursions that Ocean Voyages features aboard 70 large vessels worldwide—from the Aegean to the Caribbean to the South Pacific.

This rather complicated global operation—which has placed over 3,000 sailors on adventure cruises since 1978—is choreographed by Mary Crowley, a seasoned modern mariner. Her mission is to somehow tap the vagabond within each of us, and the voyage to Cocos Island was one example of the kind of service Ocean Voyages offers.

Astonishingly, our 1982 schooner *Victoria* was hand built by the Swedish crew at Karlstad on Lake Vanern north of Goteborg. She was scaled down by 20 percent from line drawings of a 1869 Swedish coaster that Leif Fahlgren found in the Goteborg Public Library. Leif and his friends set out to loft and craft this special ship, each bringing to the task some particular skill. Leif and Christer Robbinson welded her aluminum hull. Bjorn Hertz handled the electronics. Gunnar Aberg was the rigger and fashioned her massive spars of laminates of Swedish spruce. Lars Andersson crafted the joinery within *Victoria*'s lush interior using Brazilian mahogany. Everything (everything!) they either refashioned from used parts or built by hand. They constructed the ship's refrigeration, for instance, by marrying a cast-off compressor with some eutectic plates within insulated boxes. They even made their own turnbuckles. Her most impressive feature was the huge table on her raised afterdeck where we gathered day and night to read, write, eat, and talk about subjects of towering magnitude (like children and politics). All of this care and time and intellectual energy was invested in a vessel stout enough for three transatlantic crossings.

One way to judge a charter is by how well you eat and how well you sleep. Aboard *Victoria*, we accomplished both handsomely. Kevin Burke, our main cook and divemaster, prepared a lavish meal every evening—steaks, stuffed wahoo, filet mignon, coq au vin, cutlets, stuffed pork chops, lobster, finished off with a liqueur and a bowl of orange sherbet (in the tropics!)—just as the sun turned the western sky into a burning azure. And to rest at night, we usually pulled our mattresses up on deck to escape the heat—nodding off beneath the comforting presence of the Big Dipper and the Southern

Cross, the deck angled a satisfying 10 degrees and our progress augmented by a gentle thrum of diesel far below.

At the end of a charter, you take home with you a collection of moments. Our moments began accumulating from the morning we boarded in Puntarenas on Costa Rica's west coast (after a memorable train ride down through the mountains from San Jose) to the time we returned on a reciprocal heading five days later stopping off for a snoop through the islands in the Gulf of Nicoya.

We climbed to the waterfall at Bahia Iglesias, which we could see from the decks of *Victoria*, and later dove with Kevin to a cave at 140 feet filled with lobster, descending past underwater mountains and deep caverns that sheltered the houndfish and needlefish and snapper and jacks. We roused the white tip shark from their slumbers on the sugar-sand bottom of the Pacific, and they rose to meet us.

We watched our three Cocos guards go about their morning routine from our anchorage at Wafer Bay—no reveille, no close-order drill, or snap inspection. They tumbled from their tin hut, spit on the generator and gave it a kick, and took up their arms for a wild-pig hunt along the gravel beach.

We lay on the deck after one of Kevin's fabulous buffet lunches and consumed Dick Francis thrillers like so many cupcakes.

We snagged a marlin on a trolling rig and watched this huge fishtail walk across our wake (each of us quietly pleased to have the line snap).

We marveled at our Swedish crew for their serenity and their sense of cooperation. When a job had to be done, regardless of what is was, it was finished with scarcely a word. From the supreme navigator and rhumba dancer, Leif, to Gunnar, the smiling rigger, all seemed united in their devotion to the ship. It was remarkable and valuable to watch five men proceed through the world with such unfailing equanimity.

And when we headed back toward civilization, we watched during dinner as Cocos receded into the mists—a good place for it. Sheltered. Waiting.

Adapted (with permission) from an article by Tim Cole first published in Yachting *magazine.*

Setting the Pace

Womantrek

Most world travelers like nothing better than to wax poetic about the exotic peoples they've met or the magnificent art and scenery they've seen. But Bonnie Bordas, owner of Seattle-based Womantrek—a six-year-old adventure travel company for women—says her best memories are of the women whose lives have been changed by the trips she organizes.

"We had a woman on our '84 bicycling-in-Mongolia trip who was recently widowed," Bordas remembers. "She decided at age 63 to bicycle, even though she hadn't been on a bike since she was a kid and didn't own one. Her husband had died four months earlier. She was somewhat sullen, quiet at the beginning. She rode every distance, although she fell off her bike in the sand a couple of times. As the trip progressed she became more lively, healed by being and talking with other women.

"We've had other women come back and change careers. One was a nurse for 15 years who'd always wanted to quit. She went on a China trip, thought about things, and a year later she became a sociologist," Bordas says.

All kinds of women join Womantrek adventures, ranging in age from their early twenties to late sixties, some are veteran explorers while others are camping or going abroad for the first time. Many are high-powered businesswomen who want to get away from the stress of their jobs.

Sharon Lester, the only female custom home builder in Nashville, Tennessee, and a member of last summer's llama pack trip in Washington state's North Cascades, put it this way: "I work with men all day. It gets lonely. Traveling with women for a week sounded invigorating."

Group travel can be a freeing experience, as women get out of their caretaker roles for a short time. It has been a welcome change for Judy Flynn, a Seattle sculptor and a veteran of several Womantrek trips. "I feed, mother, and clothe men on a daily basis—it's good to take a rest."

Since 41-year-old Bordas—tall, lean, and fit—is herself a fresh-air junkie, most of Womantrek's excursions are energetic, outdoor adventures. Nevertheless, she makes women of all sizes and physical condition feel comfortable by establishing a slow, easy pace. Quiet and usually relaxed, her leadership is like that of a low-key mother hen. She especially watches out for first-time travelers, talking to them several times before the trip to relieve any anxiety and to make sure they are bringing the proper clothing.

Womantrek destinations and itineraries are often those that are difficult to experience as an independent traveler. About one-third of the trips are in the United States while the others are spread all over the globe. The shortest is a single day of bald-eagle watching and rafting on Washington's Skagit River. The longest is a 23-day bicycle tour of western China.

In addition, among 1989's approximately 32 offerings were: an African safari; walking tours of India, Nepal, Peru, and Greece; sea kayaking in Baja California; bicycling in China, West Africa, and Nova Scotia; llama packing in Oregon; skiing in Washington, Oregon and New Mexico; rafting through the Grand Canyon and on Idaho's Salmon River; and snorkeling in Puerto Rico. Next year a trip to the former Soviet Union is being planned.

Bordas leads several of the trips. The others are led by extremely accomplished people whom she personally selects. Treks in Nepal are led by an American woman who has lived there for 12 years, speaks the language fluently, and writes for the region's equivalent of the *Wall Street Journal*. Next year's new Sikkim trek will be led by the 48-year-old widow of the Sherpa guide who accompanied Hillary on his ascent of Mt. Everest. She runs her own trekking company.

"I think everyone who comes has a spirit of adventure about them to choose these kinds of trips," Bonnie says. "They may be a little nervous about whether they can do it, but they're very determined. They discover they can do things they thought they couldn't do. If they've only bicycled five miles in their entire life around their neighborhood, they get to China or some other country and realize they can bike 30 miles a day and feel just fine."

An important and unique component of Womantrek's cross-cultural trips is the link made with women abroad. On last year's safari in Tanzania, the group met with three different tribes. "The women were just wonderful, taking us into their dung huts, showing us their children, and trading songs with us," recalls Seattle chemist Pat Schlesinger of the morning spent in the Masai village of their guide.

Bordas began her professional involvement with the outdoors as an instructor in 1978, the last year she taught English at the George School, a private Quaker high school in Newton, Pennsylvania. A longtime wilderness enthusiast, she decided to offer a course combining the reading of adventure literature with such activities as rock climbing and orienteering. The fresh air beckoned.

She spent the next 15 months teaching survival skills to delinquent boys. If they survived 42 days in the woods, they were released from that institution. After that she joined the staff of Outward Bound's North Carolina wilderness school. While there she led more than 30 9-day backpacking and canoeing courses for women—helping build self-confidence and personal growth through progressively more challenging, yet always attainable, experiences.

By 1981 Bordas has spent three intense years as a wilderness instructor, often working in cold mountain climes for months at a time and earning only subsistence wages. It was time for another change. In 1982 Bordas followed some friends and moved west to Olympia, Washington.

"I was unemployed and having a career crisis in my mid-thirties," she explains. "I just did not know what I wanted to do. I couldn't let go of all the wonderful things that happen in the out-of-doors to people—men, women, and high-school kids. I couldn't see myself working in an office. I just couldn't see myself doing anything."

"The only inspirational thing I did for about a year and a half was to write (to) China Passage, a bicycle touring company. I told them I was the one to offer a women's bicycling tour of China. They called me on New Year's Eve in 1982, and in eight weeks I had 18 women, aged 26 to 68, signed up."

In May 1983, Bordas led the first all-women's bicycle tour of China. "That trip went to an area that probably no foreigner has ever cycled before," she remembers. "Whole towns would come out and watch us as we bicycled on our 18-speed bikes wearing helmets." About three weeks after returning, she took eight women rafting on Alaska's Tatshenshini River—also a first.

By August she'd decided to start using the name Womantrek, officially beginning her business. "It was like being in a rocket ship," Bordas says now. "And it's been nonstop ever since."

Maybe because Womantrek is already "beyond my wildest dreams," Bordas finds it hard to step back and imagine the future. Even if someday she adds several more office staff to relieve her of the day-to-day paperwork, or—thinking bigger—opens branches coast to coast and in China, certain fundamentals won't change.

"I'd always like to keep the high quality, the small numbers in the groups, and the personal attention that I give to the trips. I want to maintain these components because they are the reasons I keep getting repeat customers who say they want to travel with Womantrek for a lifetime."

Adapted (with permission) from an article by Robin J. Dunitz first published in Alaska Airlines *magazine.*

III

Cross-Referenced Indexes

The following cross-referenced indexes are designed to help you locate an organization that offers programs that meet your specific needs. The first section lists organizations by the subjects covered in their courses, seminars, or tours. Many are listed in a number of subject areas, while others are listed in only one or two. If you are interested in a particular subject, you may want to look for an organization that specializes in that field. If you have a broad range of interests, you may want to investigate organizations that offer programs in more than one area.

After you have located one or more organizations that seem to meet your needs, you can read about them before you send off for information. You will then be given more complete details about the dates, costs, and locations of the programs offered.

Subject

The subject categories listed below are diverse enough to give you at least a general idea of whether an organization offers programs that cover your areas of interest. If your specific area of interest isn't listed, look in the category that is closest to it and read about the organizations listed there. You may find one that does offer a suitable program.

BIOLOGY

The organizations included below offer programs that cover a wide range of biological subjects and may be best for those of you who have broad, general interests.

BIRDS

The organizations listed in this section all offer programs that focus on birding activities.

FAMILY ORIENTATION

While many organizations in this guide offer programs that are appropriate for the whole family, those below actively encourage family involvement in many activities.

Three Circles Center for Multicultural
   Environmental Education, 55
University of Kansas, 56
Vermont Institute of Natural Science, 56
Whistler Centre for Business and the Arts, 153
Whitefish Point Bird Observatory, 57
Yellowstone Institute, The, 82
YMCA of the Rockies, 102
Yosemite Field Seminars, 83

GEOLOGY

Few people mention geology as one of the natural sciences, but it
is a very important part of many programs. The organizations below
offer many activities that help participants understand the role of
geology in natural history.

Academy of Natural Sciences of Philadelphia, The, 44
Adirondack Park Visitor Centers, 60
American Littoral Society, 87
Austin Nature Center, 45
Big Bend Natural History Association, 60
Breazeale Interpretive Center, 45
Cabrillo Marine Museum, 45
California Academy of Sciences, 46
California State Polytechnic University, 17
Canyon Explorers Club, 88
Canyonlands Field Institute, 61
Chesapeake Bay Foundation, 89
Chet Ager Nature Center, 62
Cloud Ridge Naturalists, 62
Crow Canyon Archaeological Center, 64
Dale Fort Field Centre, 156
Denver Museum of Natural History, 48

MAMMALS

Large mammals, from whales to grizzlies, hold a special fascination for many people. The organizations below bring participants face-to-face with whales, wolves, and other large mammals.

MARINE SCIENCE

Marine science covers everything from flyfishing in northern California to a close-up study of gray whales in the Sea of Cortez. As long as programs and courses concern water and its relationship to the environment, they are included below.

NATIVE AMERICANS

Many organizations offer programs that study how Native Americans interacted with their environment and teach participants how to integrate the old ways with modern living.

OUTDOOR LEADERSHIP AND SURVIVAL TRAINING

While not really nature study as such, outdoor leadership and survival training programs do take place in the outdoors and do teach participants about how to interact and survive with nature. The organizations below all include such training in their programs.

PHOTOGRAPHY

Included in the organizations below are those that specifically teach about how to produce interesting and artistic nature photos, as well as those that offer participants an opportunity to take nature photos during other activities.

PLANTS

Plants are at the bottom of the ecological pyramid, and no other living creatures can survive without them. The organizations below offer programs that study the role of plants in relation to the natural history of an area and their importance to the environment.

RAIN FORESTS

Rain forests have become a focal point of the environmental movement in recent years, and rightly so. It is difficult to overemphasize their importance in the natural environment. Unfortunately most people associate rain forests only with the tropics and ignore the equally important temperate rain forests such as those of the western coast of North America from northern California to Alaska. The organizations below offer participants a chance to explore and learn about both tropical and temperate rain forests.

WOMEN ONLY

The organizations below are just for women. Other organizations, particularly those in the Field Institute section, also offer special "For Women Only" programs.

Region

Some organizations offer programs in many regions, while others are very limited in range. If you are more interested in a specific region than you are in a specific subject matter, then this is the section that you should first investigate. After you have discovered which group offers programs in the location you want to visit, you can look at the subject index or the main text to see whether its topics interest you.

ASIA

CANADA

CENTRAL CANADA

Central Canada covers the Prairie Provinces.

Sail North, 152

CENTRAL AMERICA

EUROPE

All the countries of Europe plus Great Britain are covered in this index.

UNITED STATES

Programs located in the United States are indexed according to the following regions: Alaska, Hawaii, Midwest, Northeast, Northwest, Rocky Mountains, Southeast, Southwest, and throughout.

ALASKA

HAWAII

MIDWEST

The Midwest includes everything to the west of the northeastern states to the Rocky Mountain region.

NORTHEAST

The Northeast is loosely defined as those states to the north of Washington, DC, that touch the Atlantic shoreline.

NORTHWEST

This region covers Washington, Oregon, and northern California.

ROCKY MOUNTAINS

This region covers all the states that the Rocky Mountains are found in with the exception of New Mexico.

SOUTHEAST

The Southeast is loosely defined as those states below Washington, DC, that extend west to the Mississippi River (although Arkansas and Louisiana are included). The Grand Bahamas and Virgin Islands are also included here.

SOUTHWEST

This region covers Texas, New Mexico, Arizona, and southern California.

American Cetacean Society, 87
American Wilderness Experience, Inc., 106
Austin Nature Center, 45
Big Bend Natural History Association, 60
Cabrillo Marine Museum, 45
Canyon Explorers Club, 88
Canyonlands Field Institute, 61
Catalina Science Semester, 17
Desert Survivors, 89
Environmental Traveling Companions, 111
Four Corners School of Outdoor Education, 66
Grand Canyon Expeditions Company, 113
Indian Nations International, 137
Island Packers, 115
Massachusetts Audubon Society, 95
Mono Lake Foundation, 91
National Outdoor Leadership School, 29
Natural History Museum of Los Angeles County, 50
Orange County Marine Institute, 51
Outdoor Semester in the Rockies, 32
Pacific Sea Fari Tours, 123
Prescott College, 33
Rio Grande Nature Center, 52
San Antonio Museum Association, 52
Santa Barbara Zoological Gardens, 54
Sierra Photographic Workshops, 138
Sunracer Photography, 139
Texas Tech University Center at Junction, 38
Tucson Audubon Society, 96

THROUGHOUT

The organizations below offer programs throughout the United States.

WORLDWIDE

The organizations below offer programs around the world on a regular basis.

College Credit

Some organizations, such as colleges and universities, give participants the option of obtaining academic credit for almost every course. Others, such as many field institutes and clubs, have made arrangements for participants to gain course credit through a cooperating university. A large number of organizations in the guide do not offer college credit for any courses or programs, but you can often make your own arrangements through a college near you if you need to.

CREDIT

The organizations below offer many credit classes on a regular basis.

POTENTIAL CREDIT

The organizations below do not generally offer credit for their programs but have arrangements with a college or university to provide credit for those participants who are interested.

The organizations not listed in the above two indexes generally do not offer credit for their programs, nor have they made arrangements with any college or university to do so. If you are interested in any of their programs and wish to obtain credit for your work, you should contact a local college or university extension service and inquire about obtaining credit through them.

Appendix

Below is a short list of books and periodicals that are concerned with various types of learning vacations. Learning vacations, adventure vacations, or a combination of the two are covered by these publications, which all add a different perspective for readers who want to learn more about this kind of travel. Some of the books are published in England and Canada and are not likely to be available in local bookstores. These publishers can be contacted through the addresses listed.

Books and Directories

Adventure Holidays: Thousands of Holidays in Britain and in 100 Countries Worldwide. David Stevens, Education Vacation Work Publications, 9 Park End Street, Oxford 0X1 1HJ, England. (Some titles from Vacation Work Publications are distributed by Writer's Digest Books in the U.S. and Henry Fletcher Services, Ltd. in Canada.)

Adventure Travel Abroad. Pat Dickerman, Adventure Guides, Inc., 36 E. 57th Street, New York, NY 10019.

Adventure Vacation Catalog. Specialty Travel Index, Simon & Schuster Inc. The Simon & Schuster Building, 1230 Avenue of the Americas, New York, NY 10020.

Adventure Vacations: From Trekking in New Guinea to Swimming in Siberia. Richard Bangs, John Muir Publications, PO Box 613, Santa Fe, NM 87504.

Directory of Low-Cost Vacations With a Difference. J. Crawford, Pilot Books, 103 Cooper Street, Babylon, NY 11702.

Directory of Study Abroad Programs & Travel Services. Deborah Hill, Renaissance Publications, 7819 Barkwood Drive, Worthington, OH 43085.

Directory of Work and Study in Developing Countries. David Leppard, Vacation Work Publications, 9 Park End Street, Oxford OX1 1HJ, England.

Green Travel Sourcebook: A Guide for the Physically Active, the Intellectually Curious, or the Socially Aware. Daniel and Sally Wiener Grotta, John Wiley & Sons, 605 Third Avenue, New York, NY 10158.

Guide to Earthtrips: Nature Travel on a Fragile Planet. Dwight Holing, Living Planet Press, 558 Rose Avenue, Venice, CA 90291.

International Directory of Youth Internships. Cynthia T. Morehouse, Learning Resources in International Studies, Suite 9A, 777 United Nations Plaza, New York, NY 10017.

Learning Traveler, Vols. 1 and 2. Gail Cohen, IIE, 809 United Nations Plaza, New York, NY 10017.

Learning Vacations: A Guide to All Season Worldwide Educational Travel. George Eisenberg, Peterson's Guides, PO Box 2123, Princeton, NJ 08543-2123.

New World of Travel. Arthur Frommer, Prentice-Hall, One Gulf & Western Plaza, New York, NY 10023.

Rainforest: A Guide to Research and Tourist Facilities at Selected Tropical Forest Sites in Central and South America. James L. Castner, Feline Press, PO Box 7219, Gainesville, FL 32605.

Teenager's Guide to Study, Travel, and Adventure Abroad. Marjorie Adoff Cohen, IIE, 809 United Nations Plaza, New York, NY 10017.

Travel and Learn: The New Guide to Educational Travel. Evelyn Kaye, Blue Penguin Publications, 147 Sylvan Avenue, Leonia, NJ 07605.

Vacation Study Abroad. Edrice Howard, Ed., IIE, 809 United Nations Plaza, New York, NY 10017.

What in the World Is Going On? Opportunities for Canadians to Work, Volunteer, or Study in Developing Countries. Ingrid Knutsen, CBIE, 85 Albert Street, Suite 1400, Ottawa, ON, Canada K1P 6A4.

Work, Study, Travel Abroad: The Whole World Handbook. Marjorie Adoff Cohen, St. Martin's Press, 175 Fifth Avenue, New York, NY 10010.

Periodicals

Directory of Alternative Travel Resources. Diane Brause, One World Travel Network, 81868 Lost Valley Lane, Dexter, OR 97431.

Great Expeditions. PO Box 8000-411, Abbortsford, BC V2S 6H1, Canada; PO Box 8000-411, Sumas, WA 98295-8000, U.S.A.

Transitions Abroad. 18 Hulst Road, PO Box 344, Amherst, MA 01004.

Travel & Leisure. 1120 Avenue of the Americas, New York, NY 10036.

Outside. 1165 North Clark Street, Chicago, IL 60610.

National Geographic Traveler. 17th & M Streets, NW, Washington, DC 20036.

Another source of information on learning about nature in nature is various state departments of education or parks and recreation in the U.S. Some (a few are listed below) compile booklets listing programs that include environmental or outdoor education components. Contact the parks and recreation and education departments in the states you are interested in to see if they have such a guide. A few examples are listed below.

California State Department of Parks and Recreation
  San Mateo Coast District
  95 Kelly Avenue
  Half Moon Bay, CA 94019
  Produce *A Catalog of Nature Walks and Classroom Programs.*

Iowa Conservation Education Council
  c/o Conservation Education Center
  RR 1, Box 53
  Guthrie Center, Iowa 50115
  Produce *A Guide to EE/Interpretive Services in Iowa* by the Iowa Association of Naturalists

Maryland Department of Education
  Division of Instruction
  200 West Baltimore Street
  Baltimore, MD 21201
  Produce *A Field Guide to Maryland Environmental Education Resources.*

About the Author

Bill McMillon is the author of three editions of *Volunteer Vacations: A Directory of Short-Term Adventures That Will Benefit You . . . And Others*. His other works include *California's Underwater State Parks: A Diver's Guide, The Old Lodges & Hotels of Our National Parks, Nature Nearby, The Archaeology Handbook*, and *101 Best Day Nature Hikes With Children in the San Francisco Bay Area*. He has published over 400 articles in both regional and national magazines.

He lives in Sebastopol, California, with his wife. He has three children.